Resilience

Coaching in Practice series

The aim of this series is to help coaching professionals gain a broader understanding of the challenges and issues they face in coaching, enabling them to make the leap from being a 'good-enough' coach to an outstanding one. This series is an essential aid for both the novice coach eager to learn how to grow a coaching practice, and the more experienced coach looking for new knowledge and strategies. Combining theory with practice, the series provides a comprehensive guide to becoming successful in this rapidly expanding profession.

Published and forthcoming titles:

Bluckert: *Psychological Dimensions to Executive Coaching*
Brockbank and McGill: *Coaching with Empathy*
Brown and Brown: *Neuropsychology for Coaches: Understanding the Basics*
Driver: *Coaching Positively*
Hawkins: *Creating a Coaching Culture*
Hay: *Reflective Practice and Supervision for Coaches*
Hayes: *NLP Coaching*
McGregor: *Coaching Behind Bars: Facing challenges and creating hope in a women's prison*
Paice: *New Coach: Reflections from a Learning Journey*
Rogers: *Developing a Coaching Business*
Sandler: *Executive Coaching: A Psychodynamic Approach*
Vaughan Smith: *Therapist into Coach*
Wildflower: *The Hidden History of Coaching*

Resilience

A Practical Guide for Coaches

Carole Pemberton

Mc Graw Hill Education Open University Press

Open University Press
McGraw-Hill Education
McGraw-Hill House
Shoppenhangers Road
Maidenhead
Berkshire
England
SL6 2QL

email: enquiries@openup.co.uk
world wide web: www.openup.co.uk

and Two Penn Plaza, New York, NY 10121-2289, USA

First published 2015

A catalogue record of this book is available from the British Library

ISBN-13: 978-0-335-26374-5
ISBN-10: 0-335-26374-7
eISBN: 978-0-335-26375-2

Library of Congress Cataloging-in-Publication Data
CIP data applied for

Typeset by Aptara, Inc.
Printed and bound by CPI Group (UK) Ltd, Croydon, CR0 4YY

Praise for this book

"The fascinating chapters on client narrative and 'Narrative Wave' alone make this a must-read for both new and more experienced coaches. Carole Pemberton explores the essential theories currently influencing resilience coaching, alongside stories from her own reflective practice in applying these and useful coaching tips."

Trevor Elkin, Leadership and Talent Development, Home Office

"The resilience of coaching clients is emerging as one of the key themes facing coaches in the 21st Century. Carole Pemberton's timely work brings together the key facets of this subject providing an understanding of what impacts on resilience for the client and the coach, before providing an overview of a range of useful interventions to apply when working on this issue with clients."

Caroline Horner, MD of the i-coach academy

"Wonderful to see a coaching book on resilience that compliments more traditional approaches with emergent thinking from the fields of mindfulness, ACT and positive psychology. Carole shows great wisdom and humility – pointing to the importance of authenticity in teaching mindfulness to others and in sharing her own learning along the way."

Mark McMordie, Director of Coaching, Coachmatch

"This is a Treasure Trove of practical, accessible and proven tools for skilled coaches. Carole has created THE definitive guide for helping people to use their enhanced resilience to achieve their potential."

Stuart Lindenfield FRSA, Head of Career and Change Management Solutions, Reed Global

"Pemberton has a rare skill – turning knowledge into power. She gives the reader the wherewithal to notice when resilience is failing in their clients. She then equips them with useful lines of inquiry and creative, practical steps they can take with their clients to move them from being stuck to taking responsibility and accessing their resources. She writes of the tricky subject of identity: often a subject tackled in dense philosophical debate: she makes it accessible, giving clear guidance in eloquent plain English about how a coach can work with their client at identity level. The work you as a coach will be able to do as a result of reading this book will be deeper and more creative. My notebook was full of tips and ideas by the time I had left the book."

Deborah Tom, Managing Director of Human Systems

For Cameron,

may you face your life adventures with resilience

Contents

Series Editor's Foreword		xi
Preface		xiii
Acknowledgements		xv
List of figures and tables		xvii
1	**What is resilience?**	1
2	**You and your resilience**	20
3	**The loss of resilience narrative**	29
4	**Coaching the narrative**	41
5	**Cognitive behavioural therapy and resilience**	52
6	**Acceptance and commitment therapy and resilience**	66
7	**Mindfulness and resilience**	80
8	**Solution-focused coaching and resilience**	95
9	**Positive psychology and resilience**	109
10	**Coaching for career resilience**	122
	Bibliography	141
	Index	147

Series Editor's Foreword

It does not take long in a coaching career before you meet a client who has been seriously rocked by events in his or her life. It could be the loss of a job, the expected death of a frail parent – but a death which is unexpectedly dismaying, an accident, illness, a severe falling out with a close friend. The incidents themselves will vary, but the human reaction will become familiar. In my own practice as an executive coach I reckon that at least a third of my clients will be experiencing some loss of resilience in the period during which I am working with them, and these clients are typically high-functioning, successful people. They will use vivid metaphors to describe their feelings at these times – they are 'unmoored' 'knocked out', 'shocked', sometimes they will talk of 'anaesthetizing' themselves with food or drink, and generally behaving in ways that are so far out of their usual pattern that they are unrecognizable to themselves. Their normal ways of coping are not working. They have *lost their mojo*. What do you do as a coach when you see this happening? Do you refer them to a therapist, knowing that very few clients will ever follow up on this suggestion? Do you listen quietly but do nothing more, wondering if maybe you have let the client down? If neither of these two extremes is desirable, then what?

Carole's book will give you two vital sets of tools for working with these clients. First, she offers a fresh and thoughtful framework for understanding what resilience is and is not – and why it has such potential for triggering feelings of being de-stabilized, especially where questions of core identity are involved. The reason this is important is that it will stop you from being as overwhelmed as your client or from having unrealistic expectations about the outcomes of the work – for instance that the client 'should just bounce back' from whatever their crisis has been.

Secondly, the book will take you step by step through a series of practical interventions, a menu of options, each with their research base and with their practicality explored. So how far is the currently fashionable concept of mindfulness helpful? How can you use some of the principles of Cognitive Behavioural Therapy? What can you borrow from Solution-focused Coaching and Positive Psychology? They all have something to contribute and this book will show you what is especially useful in these disciplines for work with clients whose resilience has temporarily vanished.

The book will also help you assess your own resilience and coping mechanisms as a coach, a reminder that we have to be firmly grounded ourselves and not distracted by our own issues when we are working in this territory with clients.

I have long wanted to have a title on this subject for the *Coaching in Practice* series. Carole Pemberton has written the book that I wish I had had when I was building my own hours as a coach and I have also learnt a lot from reading it now. Take this book seriously: it will add significantly to your confidence and competence as a coach.

Jenny Rogers
Series Editor

Preface

Clients come to coaching with their tough stuff. It can be stuff they never expected to happen and which has challenged their model of how life should be. It can be tough realizations about themselves which leave them asking 'what now?' It can be tough feedback that challenges them to change. They come with their resilience knocked and looking for answers. As coaches, we want to widen and deepen their understanding so that they are re-sourced to handle what they have been given; and yet sometimes we can feel as stuck as they are.

The starting point for this book was my own 'stuckness'. I had many years' experience as a coach, and yet one client threw me completely. I had known him for several years and coached him as his career progressed. I knew him as a successful, talented, and confident man. The person now turning up at coaching sessions was very different. He was fixated on the failings of everyone around him, as he struggled with his job. He could see no way of how things could change. The energy he could have put into sorting out his situation was instead focused on obsessive exercise regimes. After one session I wrote that I felt I was offering him a sticking plaster rather than helping him deal with the real issues. Eventually he became ill and had to take time out. When he returned, he asked to meet with me, and the word 'resilience' started to enter our conversations. He now recognized he had lost his in the months before his illness, and he wanted to ensure it did not happen again. My disappointment in myself as a coach, combined with a curiosity to understand more of what resilience was, re-energized our work. What I learnt from him fed into work with other clients, and eventually led me to doctoral research on resilience coaching.

I wanted to understand more of an issue that psychologists, psychiatrists, and development experts had studied for many years. I wanted to know what conclusions drawn from studies of individuals outside of work settings held true for adults working in corporate environments. The more I read, the more I became convinced that the focus on measuring resilience was insufficient. There are many questionnaires that assess resilience, as though it is a fixed capacity. However, I found little on how coaches can work with clients when their resilience has abandoned them, and a quality they normally have access to is less available.

This book is the output of my desire to do better for my clients. It is written for coaches at any stage of their development who would like a deeper understanding of what resilience is, and how to recognize its loss. It is for those who are looking for input on different ways in which to work with resilience gaps. The book does not argue for one approach over any other, but lays out the choices you have, and when you might use them. Central to the book is an interest in understanding the narrative that a client brings, and how you can work with that narrative to better understand what it is that needs addressing in order to move forward.

I am writing for those who want to help their clients build resilience resources to deal with the relentless demands of their lives. It is also written for times when a particular event has hit your client hard. It is designed to support career coaching, by encouraging clients to look at the being of resilience and not just the doing of actions to ensure marketability.

Finally, this book is for you as a coach. Coaching is demanding work. There are times when clients test your resilience and you may lose confidence, optimism, and purpose. Coaches can display the very qualities we see in our clients. By reading this book, I hope you are better resourced to understand your own resilience, so that you can better support others in developing theirs.

If you find this book useful when you are working with tough stuff, or you wish to share approaches that you use in your resilience coaching, then I would love to hear from you.

Carole Pemberton
carole.pemberton@coachingtosolutions.com
www.coachingtosolutions.com

Acknowledgements

Jenny Rogers, the series editor of *Coaching in Practice*, is the catalyst for this book. If she had not sat in on a session I was giving at a research conference, the book would never have been written. Alongside her are Dr Annette Fillery-Travis and Dr Mary Hartog from Middlesex University. They supported me in starting – and then ensuring I completed – my doctorate. The many clients who have brought me their resilience issues throughout the years have taught me everything I know. In particular, those individuals who were part of my research project have my gratitude. Alex Burgess of ABTraining kept me fit while I spent long hours sitting at the computer. When my writing resilience was deserting me, an exercise session often released my best thoughts. My biggest thanks and love go to Bill, who without ever complaining did all the hundred things I was failing to do while absorbed in writing this book; and Cameron for ensuring I kept a sense of perspective on what really matters.

List of figures and tables

Figures

Figure 1.1   The three-factor model of resilience   9
Figure 4.1   The Narrative Wave™   43
Figure 4.2   A holding wave pattern   45
Figure 4.3   The coach in the resilience coaching process   46
Figure 6.1   The values dartboard   77
Figure 8.1   Creating a scale   100
Figure 8.2   Your resilience template   103
Figure 9.1   The Positivity Ratio Checklist   118
Figure 10.1   The Career Resilience Model   130
Figure 10.2   The Career Butterfly Model   133
Figure 10.3   The Career Butterfly in Action   133

Tables

Table 5.1   Example of ABC   60
Table 5.2   Challenging the ABC   60
Table 10.1   PESTLE your career   132

1   What is resilience?

A community deals stoically with the aftermath of severe flooding, a football team grabs victory at the last minute after being outplayed, the luxury soap market remains buoyant during recession, and a bank gets its ATMs operating quickly after an IT failure. What links them? They have all been described in the media as resilient. This word is used so widely that it is important to start by asking: What does resilience mean in the context of coaching? How does its lack show up in your clients, and what do you need to know in order to be able to meet their needs? This chapter will answer those questions. It will look at what is known about resilience from the wealth of research on the subject: the degree to which it is genetic or acquired, and how it differs from related conditions such as post-traumatic stress disorder (PTSD) and 'burnout'. It will unpick the label, to enable you to better understand the different capacities that contribute to resilience, so that you can recognize different needs in your clients.

What is resilience?

A useful place to start is the origin of the word 'resilience' in the physical sciences. Here it is seen as the ability of a material to return to its original state after it has been bent or stretched. It is like an elastic band that can stretch to accommodate objects of different shapes and sizes, and then return to its original form when released. It is the ability of a suspension bridge to move slightly in response to the weight of traffic but then return to a stable state. It is the carbon fibre of the pole vault bending under the weight of the athlete as they rise into the air but not breaking. The word comes from the Latin root *resili*, meaning the ability to spring back, in relation to the capacity of plants to adapt themselves to different conditions. If you have ever seen a flower growing through concrete, or a tree growing at a seemingly impossible angle from a crumbling cliff face, you have witnessed resilience in nature.

In relation to human behaviour, then, resilience is:

The capacity to remain flexible in our thoughts, feelings, and behaviours when faced by a life disruption, or extended periods of pressure, so that we emerge from difficulty stronger, wiser, and more able.

Central to resilience is the ability to remain adaptive when under strain and to re-orientate to the new situation. It is the ability to reconfigure your day when travel plans go awry, or to recognize that a presentation is going badly and rapidly change it to align with the audience's interest rather than ploughing on with what you had prepared. It is accepting that the film you hoped to see is sold out, and quickly coming up with a Plan B, rather than seeing your evening as ruined.

It is a quality we draw on all the time, but there are occasions when our resilience is severely tested. Sometimes it comes in the form of life events such as the death of parents, a partner or a much-loved friend. It can come in the ending of an important relationship, whether we are seventeen or seventy. A leader can accept the case for restructuring a business and its translation into role redundancy, but still be completely derailed when it happens to them. Life continuously tests our resilience, and no one is immune.

Equally, our resilience is tested when the pressures are relentless and there is no end in sight. A Chartered Institute of Personnel and Development (CIPD) (2014a) *Megatrends* report claimed that working hours were not becoming longer, but that people were being asked to meet ever-tighter deadlines with fewer resources. When that has been the case year after year, this way of working becomes the norm, and resilience can become stretched to the point where it cannot spring back. Elasticity becomes spent, and is replaced by a rigidity of thinking and behaving, accompanied by emotions that undermine confidence in self and connection to others. It becomes harder to remain motivated, and commitment to work and colleagues shrinks.

What resilience is not

A common metaphor associated with resilience is 'bounceback'. This is the idea that individuals are rubber balls who get pushed to the ground but spring back up. It's the 'pick yourself up' approach to life. This image denies the reality of working through difficulties. Anyone who has faced a major obstacle in life will have been changed by it. They move forward with a different perspective, with changed values, and with hard-won learning. The word 'bounceback' does not reflect how tough that process can be. In working with clients, I talk instead of how they can work through a difficulty, so that they move forward better resourced for the next challenge that life throws at them.

Frequently, I hear celebrities talk of how they have dealt with a headline-grabbing setback with the phrase, 'what doesn't kill you makes you stronger'. It is their assertion that they are now toughened by what life has dealt them. They see themselves as invulnerable. This is not resilience. Resilience is not a guarantee of armoured protection. However much is learned from adversity, we are still open to being knocked by the unexpected. Dealing with a major illness doesn't offer immunity against being knocked sideways by a minor car accident. Or being pragmatic in the face of redundancy doesn't inoculate against being floored by the death of a parent, even though it was long expected. The 'what doesn't kill you...' line suggests heroic powers, whereas the person may now simply be driven by a bitter determination never to be touched by anyone or anything again. That is not resilience. Resilience is about being open to learning and growth, being able to take risks because of a sense of being able to deal with the consequences of that risk. Resilience does not protect us from setback, but it ensures we are able to manage our way through it.

Recognizing when resilience goes

Your client may not understand the term resilience, or may have an understanding of the word that is very different from a textbook definition, so in looking for evidence of resilience loss, I look for signs of change they are noticing in themselves. A person who normally presents confidently reports that they are avoiding challenging situations because their trust in their actions has gone. A leader who is relied on to take decisions reports that his team is becoming frustrated with his procrastination. A manager tells me that his emotions and thoughts within work are overwhelmingly negative when he knows his team needs him to show positivity and confidence at a difficult time. A senior leader reports that her ability to operate her emotional filter and control what leaks out has gone, and she observes herself behaving with a volatility that she cannot control. A sociable extrovert admits that they no longer meet up with colleagues after work, or are avoiding social time with friends, because they fear that negative feelings about themselves will be heightened by being in contact with others who are seeing the world differently. In a coaching session, I notice that a client is fixated on one solution, and since that is not possible they are stuck, whereas previously I have experienced them as resourceful and creative. Or they talk repeatedly of how the world/others should be, rather than working with the reality of what is. They keep using the same approach even though it does not work, because they cannot flex their thinking. Some clients tell me their anger is easily triggered and they swear when normally they would not. Others report they are using food, drink, drugs or mindless TV to dull their senses, even though they know those responses do not help. They have stopped exercising even though they know it makes them feel better. Instead, they see themselves as isolated both from the self they normally access and from others. There is no blueprint for how lack of resilience shows up, but each client will have their own template of how they react when their resilience is being overwhelmed.

Case study: Recognizing a client's template

James presented as extremely self-confident. He was an acknowledged world leader in his area of expertise, and had willingly accepted voluntary redundancy in the belief that he would quickly find a new role.

When success did not come quickly, and he found himself regularly coming second in selection processes, he was thrown. He became fixated on how others had failed him. His boss must not have written a good enough reference. The selection process was flawed. At the same time, he reported that he could not sleep at night, and when he woke in the early hours his brain flooded with thoughts about what he should have said that would have led to a different outcome.

He eventually acknowledged that he had lost confidence. This was a big admission for him. He could not answer the question 'who am I?', since he had no sense of himself if he wasn't the person whose status was signalled by his job title. He did not want to go out into the world and put himself forward for further rejection. Instead, he spent hours crafting his profile on LinkedIn, so that it would signal his importance.

James had not learnt resilience because it had never before been tested.

He held the idea that people should want him for his brain power alone, and when they did not he was lost, because his identity was linked to his intellect. It was the expert identity which he held onto tightly and which he took into interviews, even when the interviewers wanted to see the leader in him. It was only when he was helped to realize that he had other identities to call on that were more useful, that his resilience started to return.

Some clients recognize that they are losing their resilience, but for those who do not, it will be you as the coach who holds that mirror up to them. You notice that the way in which they talk about themselves and their situation has changed. You listen to their account and it does not feel real to you. You sense that they are avoiding facing reality. You notice that they present the situation with a certainty that only allows for their interpretation. You are struck by the power of emotion that they are directing towards individuals who they blame for their plight. You become aware that any attempt to move them towards solution-finding is immediately blocked and discounted. They appear tired, less cared for or are visibly putting on or losing weight. When you notice this, you have the opportunity to feed back what you are noticing so as to open up the possibility of their recognizing that for the moment their resilience has left them. If they recognize the mirror you are holding, the opportunity is there for you to begin addressing their resilience with them. Before you do so, it is important that you understand what it is that contributes to resilience.

What do we know about resilience?

As coaches working with talented, able adults in situations that are not life-threatening, it is relevant to know that most research has been conducted with children living with particular life difficulties. Research has focused on children with a single challenge such as a parent with mental health issues, or who are living with multiple deprivations such as poor parenting, poverty, poor housing or issues of abuse. In contrast, when adults have been the focus it has often been as survivors of extreme conditions, such as prisoners of war and internees in concentration camps, or as adults living with life-threatening conditions such as AIDS. Until recently, little attention has been given to the resilience of high achievers within work environments. However, the history of resilience research is important because it deepens our understanding of what contributes to an individual's resilience profile.

The history of thinking on resilience has moved through three distinct phases:

- *Trait theory*: resilience as a capacity that is linked to innate personality factors.
- *Protection*: resilience as access to factors in the individual's environment that provide protection against the impact of difficulty.
- *Learned*: resilience as a capacity that is acquired through learning from difficulty.

Trait theory

Resilience was initially thought of as a personality trait, which you either did or did not have. This approach saw resilience as something that is stable within a personality and will always be available to those who are gifted with being resilient. This was the conclusion of early researchers, who believed that the reason that some children did better than others, after starting with similar deficits, was a genetic advantage. Such children are hardwired to be able to deal with life's challenges in ways that are not available to others. This view of resilience as a personality trait underpins many psychometric questionnaires. It is attractive to organizations because it suggests that individuals can be selected for their resilience, and this will provide some predictability in how they will respond to pressures.

Support for trait theory also comes from recent studies in neuroscience, which argue that genetic factors can explain why some people are able to deal more easily with the slings and arrows of life. Neuroscientists are suggesting that differences in the brain explain differences in how we respond to stress. One difference is in how we produce serotonin. Serotonin is the neurotransmitter that is associated with feelings of tranquillity, calm and well-being. Manipulating serotonin so that it is more available to particular brain cells is the basis of many anti-depressants. What neuroscience has now shown is that some individuals have a variant of the 5HTT gene that produces serotonin. They produce more serotonin than the rest of us, and so present as more optimistic, regardless of the situation they are in.

In contrast, someone with a variant of the 2-adrenoreceptor gene, which is responsible for the production of the stress hormone adrenaline, will have a higher base level of that hormone. They will respond more strongly to any stress in their environment, and it will take longer for their stress level to settle down. The amygdala is the part of the brain that is central to our emotional responses. It fuels our flight or fight response to stressful situations. How the amygdala functions is influenced by the neuropeptide Y gene. One of the roles of the gene is to reduce anxiety, but with one variant of the gene there is increased activity leading to heightened anxiety being linked to a stressful experience. To add further complexity, neuroscience has now established that we are neurally plastic, and are capable of learning throughout our lives, by making new connections. However, some of us have greater neuroplasticity than others. Some of our clients will easily make new connections – whether of thought or behaviour – while others will need more practice before that becomes possible.

Consider the possible differences in how a client may present for coaching. Annie and John are both made redundant, at a mid-career stage. Annie is gifted with higher than average levels of serotonin, above average neural plasticity, and has the normal variants of the genes linked to adrenaline and the creation of emotional meaning. John, in contrast, has the gene variants that result in higher levels of adrenaline and greater activation of his amygdala. He is less neurally plastic. Neither they nor you are aware of these genetic differences, but coaching the two of them is very different. Annie may present as stressed in the immediate aftermath of the event, but is then able to restore equilibrium to her stress levels and access her cognitive powers to examine the emotional meaning she created in the immediate aftermath of job loss. Her natural optimism provides the energy to want to move on, and she is open to experimentation and doing new things. Very quickly as a coach you will be working on how to develop her plan for her future. In contrast, John is overwhelmed by the stress of the event for far longer. He may only be able to access his emotional responses, and from this he creates a narrative that makes it impossible for him to conceive that he has a future. He finds it difficult to imagine he could do anything other than what he has already done, and cites his age as a reason for the impossibility of change. John is every bit as intelligent as Annie, but the process of recovery will be longer, and will be best helped by a coach who can both help him reduce his stress and anxiety levels and can pace with his speed of learning.

At face value, trait theory holds up. We all know people who appear able to deal with whatever life throws at them and remain upright. They may well be genetically blessed, but even those who argue for the role of genetics in resilience acknowledge that genetics play only a part. Studies of twins show that between 32 and 38 per cent of behaviour can be explained by inherited factors. Genetics play a part, but they are only one part of the story.

Protection

The second wave of resilience research looked beyond genetics to identifying conditions, which, if present or absent, would explain different outcomes. In a ground-breaking thirty-year longitudinal study of 698 Hawaiian children living in a community of multiple deprivations, Werner and Smith concluded that while there was some support for trait theory, in that those that did best were more optimistic, more autonomous, more self-confident, and were intelligent, there were two other equally important factors.

The first of these was the availability of parental warmth. Regardless of their economic circumstances, they had in the words of mid twentieth-century child development expert John Bowlby, 'secure attachment'. Their parents had been able to give them the security that they were loved and provided clear consistent rules, so that they had a sense of trust in how the world operated. They had learnt that when they were anxious, worried or upset they would be reassured. Over time they developed that capacity for themselves, so that when they went out into the world they had an internalized sense that they could manage their way through difficulty. Secondly, they had access to support. Even where parents were not able to provide secure attachment, those who fared best were able to find someone who would provide support, and help them develop a sense of purpose that was not available in the family. That person could be a teacher, youth worker, church leader or grandparent. Their role was to signal to the child that they believed in them and their possibilities. The outcome was that protected children developed a sense of purpose in their lives and a determination to do better than their backgrounds would predict.

The place of purpose in resilience is a recurrent finding of research studies. With purpose, individuals have a compass to direct their goals, and to keep them on track when they are faced with difficulty. It fuels determination, and the direction of energy. When purpose goes, individuals are more vulnerable to the loss of resilience. Conversely, some individuals find their resilience when it has been blown away by a life tragedy, through creating a purpose from that event. I have worked with clients who by creating a charity following the death of a child have found some meaning in what is otherwise meaningless, or through campaigning for more resources for a life-limiting illness, have died with a sense that their life experience is meaningful.

Seeing resilience as the product of more than personality opens up space for its development. By recognizing that the conditions around an individual are important, as coaches we can use that knowledge to signal our belief in our clients, and to explore the issue of purpose as a catalyst for recovery.

Resilience as a process

A third wave of researchers viewed resilience as a capacity that develops over time in response to learning. Rather than resilience levels being fixed, there is a continuum between resilience and vulnerability along which we constantly move. Where an individual sits at any time will be shaped by the interplay between the protection available to them and the relationship between the individual and the event. Seeing resilience as a process positions it as something that is largely learnt through encountering stressors and gaining confidence and competence in dealing with them. In this approach, our resilience grows over our lifespan. It is not a special quality available to a few. It is, according to child development expert Ann Masten, 'ordinary magic': something we learn through dealing with the demands of living. Seeing it as largely learnt highlights why some of the most able people can be the least resilient when faced with difficulty. Having always succeeded can mean that those labelled as 'talented' are sometimes the least prepared for dealing with deviations from what they have come to expect. The person who has always sat in the high potential/ high performance box of the talent grid may be the least equipped for finding a way through when the route they have followed veers off track. Our work as coaches is to help them to acquire the learning from disappointment that will equip them for the future.

Seeing resilience as largely learnt from experience does not protect us against being destabilized, but it does mean that we have learning to help us manage the stress reaction, so that it will be short-lived. It also means that the person can continue functioning in many areas of their life, while working through a difficulty in a particular area. It is that particularity of focus that separates loss of resilience from other stress-related conditions. A client may have lost resilience in respect of one aspect of their life, but still be psychologically healthy and continuing to perform in others.

Working with all three themes

In working with your clients, it is valuable to be able to hold those three themes in mind, as together they explain how your client has come to create their own resilience model (Figure 1.1).

Figure 1.1   The three-factor model of resilience

To understand the relative contribution of each theme to your client's model, you could ask the following questions:

- How optimistic or pessimistic a person would you describe your-self as naturally being?
- How would your friends or family describe how you deal with setbacks?
- When you have setbacks, how easy do you find it to let go and move on?
- What challenges did you have to deal with in your early years?
- What helped you deal with those challenges?
- Who were the people who helped you to believe in your potential?
- What has been the biggest life challenge you have faced?
- What have you learnt from dealing with that challenge that you continue to use in your life?
- Have you ever been blown sideways by a life event?
- How did you get yourself through it?

Loss of resilience as loss of access to identity

Psychological research has looked at what shapes resilience. As a coach, I am equally interested in what causes my clients to lose resilience. It was that interest that fuelled my research. In analysing participants' written and spoken narratives (see Chapters 3 and 4 for more details), it emerged that the loss of resilience was linked to loss of access to an identity that was key to their sense of self. It was not the event in itself that was desta-bilizing. They were unsettled by their view of themselves in relation to the event. In explaining what had happened to them, they had created a narra-tive in which they ascribed themselves an identity. That identity could be one of being unwanted, a victim, unloved, unprotected, vulnerable, scared child or old and discounted. Because the identity that normally supported them was of being wanted, a winner, loved, cared for, invulnerable, adult or dynamic, they were thrown by discovering the co-existence of this other identity. It was their acceptance of this newly exposed alternative identity as now holding the truth about them that was undermining their resilience and preventing them from accessing both their own resources and other identities that could help them through difficulty.

Resilience and resiliency

There is an additional distinction to be made: that between resilience and resiliency. Resilience is sometimes approached as though it is a bank account that has a balance figure that can be drawn upon when needed. This is seen in questionnaires that tell me how confident, decisive, creative or able to manage my emotions I am. The score is offered as a predictor as to how I am likely to behave when facing a tough time. What this approach ignores is the variability that comes from context. Resiliency is the degree to which you are able to put that credit balance into action. Resiliency explains why a client will remember a time when they were experiencing enormous pressures, but kept going because they had a manager who signalled believing in and valuing them, even when mistakes were made. That same person tells you the pressures on them now are less and yet they are crumpling because their manager is focusing on what is not going well, and is signalling a lack of belief in them. Separating out resiliency from resilience allows us to explore with clients when they experience themselves as more and less resilient in action, what shapes those differences, and how that influences their behaviour.

Our clients are not children

While the experiences of children are helpful, they cannot fully explain the experiences of adults. We do not know if a 35-year-old woman working in a corporate environment will access the same protectors, or has acquired the same learning, as a 10-year-old girl in a refugee camp. It is useful, therefore, to look at work with adults in order to understand what is similar and what is different.

Studies of adults in the work environment have largely focused on areas such as social work and health care. Those studies have been interested in how individuals who are experiencing relentless pressures stay strong. Being under such pressures can mean a loss of connection to the purpose of one's work. It can reduce willingness to persist when faced by difficulty, or can mean losing a sense of being part of a team with shared goals and responsibilities. Such reactions make sense in terms of individuals looking to find ways of protecting themselves in an environment that does not seem to be offering protection.

It is only recently that researchers have shown an interest in the resilience of high achievers and what we can learn from those who need resilience to reach the top. Focusing on Olympic gold medal winners, the sports psychologists David Fletcher and Mustafa Sarkar reported on interviews with Olympians over the last thirty years. They concluded that although Olympians shared many of the trait and protective factors found in studies of children, they have two additional distinguishing markers. They look at difficulties as opportunities to learn, and they are able to manage their thoughts. Whatever difficulties they face, they are able to hold onto a larger sense of their own 'OKness', rather than being defined by the immediate setback. This enables them to be open to learning from difficulty. They also have the ability to notice their thoughts and manage them, rather than being trapped by them. They have a mindful approach to noticing thoughts, and are able to apply a cognitive approach to interrogating those thoughts to assess their value in relation to their goals.

Olympians are unusual. Just being an Olympian suggests the possession of qualities that mark them out. They are not working within corporate structures. They may be part of a team, but the team exists to support them. Their goals are fixed. Their performance is managed with forensic attention to detail with a focus on ensuring success. It is important to look more closely at the world executives live in to get a better understanding of resilience at play in work.

Corporate high achievers and resilience

A small number of studies have looked at how leaders of organizations remain resilient over time, when inevitably their resources are tested. While many of the findings reinforce our three resilience themes of genetics, protective factors, and learning, there are additional nuances. Interviewees in a study that encompassed politicians, surgeons, senior police officers, and academics revealed they were also active in their approach to learning from difficulty. They reflected on what past experience had taught them and created space in the midst of tough times to reflect on themselves in action. They targeted their energies on what they could control, and consciously ensured that they had things other than work in their lives, no matter how demanding the situation. It was that contrast that enabled them to keep a sense of perspective. In a study of twenty-five business leaders, the executive coach Jenny Campbell coined the term Resilience Engine™ to describe the interplay between the individual's personal resources as input, their focus on an external goal as a driving force to output, and between the two the intervening variable of their adaptive capacity. It is that adaptive capacity which is fuelled by pacing their energies, refreshing themselves, and keeping perspective that is as important to their resilience as their personal qualities and commitment to a goal.

Career resilience: an additional perspective

There is one final perspective that is important for coaches – that of career resilience. While writers on resilience have focused on the adaptive capacity within an individual, career writers are interested in how equipped the individual is to adapt to the vicissitudes of the labour market. The focus has been on action. (For further detail, see Chapter 10.) Since many clients come for coaching because of career issues, career resilience has a distinct place in resilience coaching in relation to developing the ability of the client to take on behaviours that will increase their marketability. They may need to be helped to let go of established skills and to open up to new learning. They may need to be challenged with the logic of emerging labour market trends and its meaning for their career options. They may need to learn how to self-market when they have always relied on others to market their talents. Coaching is focused on equipping the individual to survive and thrive in a changing marketplace. Career resilience can be linked to the idea of resilience as proactively building self-protection.

The different lenses we need for working with resilience

The needs that our clients bring to us ask that we work with resilience in different ways. Consider a client who has been out of the job market for a while. He does not know how to begin the process of job search in a world of social media, and finds it impossible to think about himself other than how he was defined in his last role. His need is to be able to align himself to the reality of the world he is now re-entering. Or a client who is exhausted from taking on too much because she believes that is what it takes to be valued – she needs to learn how to challenge her own assumptions. Or a client who has had a bad year that has dented his self-belief, and needs help in letting go of the story he is now carrying. It is important as a coach that we do not just know what resilience is, but that we recognize the different needs our clients bring with them in relation to their own resilience. These needs encompass:

- *Building protection* – through taking action;
- *Building capacity* – through developing resilience skills;
- *Building renewal* – through being helped to use the learning from difficulty to move forward.

How resilience differs from post-traumatic stress disorder and burnout

Resilience is something that we all possess to some degree, and its daily use helps us retain stability in our psychological functioning. There are times when we lose access to it, but that is a temporary state before we regain stability. However, as coaches we need to be able to distinguish between when the loss is more than temporary, and when our capacity for helping our client move forward is inadequate. In particular, it is important to differentiate between resilience, and post-traumatic stress disorder and 'burnout'.

Post-traumatic stress disorder

Resilience loss is experienced in relation to normal (if unwelcome) life experiences. Post-traumatic stress disorder (PTSD) is different. It occurs when a person is exposed to the abnormal, and experiences a direct threat to their life or their psychological integrity. It is not normal to be living in daily fear of your life because of being caught in a war zone. It is not normal to experience a terrorist attack, or to be kidnapped, attacked at random or raped. It is not normal to kill another person in battle and to witness the consequences of that killing. It is because these experiences are outside of normal human experience that individuals are ill-equipped to process them. There is no prior learning to draw on.

For anyone exposed to such threats, their model of how the world operates is torn up. It is no longer safe and predictable. It is unsafe and unknowable, and basic assumptions about themselves and the world are shaken. A good caring person can be behind the wheel of a car that kills a cyclist. Or a woman who prides herself on being cautious is raped by someone they trusted. Or a protective parent is unable to save their child from drowning. It is because the event disrupts our view of our self in the world, and there is no learning or protection that we can call on, that according to PTSD experts Peter Hodgkinson and Michael Stewart, our brain has to find its own solution. Its answer is to choose between one of three options: reliving, avoiding or increased arousal.

Reliving

When an individual is caught in reliving, they will have recurrent and distressing recollections of the event, which can occur at any time. They may regularly dream about what happened to them and wake in a distressed state. They may relive the event over and over again, experiencing the same thoughts and feelings as those when it occurred. They may respond to a similar event happening to someone else, or to the anniversary of their event by becoming distressed.

Avoidance

When the brain chooses to avoid, the most common reaction is to avoid talking about the event. It is the reaction of many soldiers who have seen the unimaginable in warfare, and never talk of it with their family. If they do mention it, they numb their emotional response and talk as though it has had no impact on them. They may avoid any situation that reminds them of the event, refusing to watch television programmes that touch on their experience, and reject invitations to be involved in memorial events. To their family they may appear detached and emotionally cool. They have chosen to stay separate from others because the emotional cost of attachment is too high.

Increased arousal

When the brain reacts by increasing arousal, it is as though the individual is in a permanent state of readiness for danger. They report a sense of hyper-vigilance, such as having a strong sense of smell after being caught in a fire and dreading firework displays, or avoiding crowds after having been trapped trying to get out of a building. While these responses are understandable, the vigilance can manifest as a startled response towards any stimuli associated with the trauma, such as an ambulance siren or the sight of a police horse. The arousal of their emotional senses can lead to unpredictable outbursts of anger, or a sense of constantly needing to be alert can prevent them from being able to concentrate.

As coaches, it is important to recognize these symptoms when displayed by clients, and also to acknowledge that we may not be adequately equipped to deal with them. Such symptoms are often revealed because the client feels safe enough to talk about something which hitherto they have avoided acknowledging, or they make a link between a current issue and their past trauma. Their trust, however, does not mean we have the necessary specialist skills.

Case study: Recognizing PTSD

Eleanor is a career coach working with police officers leaving the service and wanting to plan the next stage of their lives. Many of the officers have been subject to physical danger and have seen colleagues killed. The culture is strongly male. Ostensibly Eleanor's role is to help them think through their career future. Often she finds herself faced with men crying as they talk about events that have had a profound effect on them. Many have failed marriages, and admit that they are devoid of feeling for others. Some own up to anger and even physical abuse in response to their inability to deal with thoughts and feelings that at times are overwhelming. They feel safe enough with Eleanor to open up and admit a desire to rid themselves of their thoughts, so that they can be at ease with themselves.

Eleanor can listen and can acknowledge their courage in speaking out, but she is not equipped to work through the issues with them. She refers them to specialist psychologists trained in the skills of desensitization: skilled practitioners who can help them begin the therapy they have avoided, often for many years. Eleanor has helped them bring the trauma into the open, but she cannot work with them on letting go of the trauma.

While working with PTSD is a specialist skill, coaches can be involved in helping clients to recognize their need for help. They can do this by listening closely to the words the client uses when talking about an abnormal stressor, so as to discuss with them how best to move forward. Nohreen Tehrani is an expert on trauma. From her work with trauma victims, she offers pointers on language clues that can signal the presence of PTSD.

When reliving, clients use visual language and speak of images that come to mind when they think of the event. You may notice them looking up as they talk, as they visualize the memory. Clients may speak of dreaming about the event often, and may even talk about the event in the present tense, even though it occurred many years previously.

When avoiding, clients may speak of the event but as though it happened to someone else. There is an emotional distance that is at odds with what they are describing. They acknowledge the event and then quickly add that they try not to think about it, or that it is not important. They avoid certain situations, however tenuous a link they have with the event. They may use humour to diminish the trauma, but the power of the avoidance is palpable.

With arousal, clients describe how smells or sounds can make them relive the event. You notice that although they are talking about the event calmly, their body is becoming tense. They speak of difficulty getting to sleep or staying asleep, which has lasted for some time and was not experienced prior to the trauma.

Burnout

Burnout is different from PTSD. Where PTSD is a stress reaction to the abnormal that can occur in any part of a person's life, 'burnout' is a particular stress reaction to work. It manifests when the personality needs of the individual collide with an environment that rewards excessive commitment to work. Tim Casserley, whose own burnout led him to research the subject, describes it graphically as a toxic combination of the personality traits of highly ambitious, driven individuals finding an addictive outlet in organizations that make high demands of its talent. Those demands are both initially personally rewarding but ultimately destructive.

Herbert Freudenberger first coined the term 'burnout' in 1974. He positioned it as a chronic affliction of the overachiever. Although people talk of being 'burnt out' after an intense and demanding period of work, they usually recover their energies after a holiday, or even by working on a different assignment. Psychologists, however, see 'burnout' as a distinct condition that develops over time. It is not a reaction to one event, and it will usually be unacknowledged by the individual until a physical crisis occurs.

Burnout builds slowly, but its key feature is that in order to burn out, a fire needs to be burning, a fire that is fuelled by excessive working. It is only when the fire is raging that the individual begins to recognize that they are being singed. The symptoms of burnout include clients talking of extreme exhaustion to the point where they struggle to get out of bed in the morning. They will speak of feeling inadequate in their role, despite giving every hour of their life to it. They may disclose that they become tearful in response to small triggers, or break down readily in coaching sessions. They may even boast of long periods of working without sleep fuelled by drink or drugs. They may have physical symptoms, such as digestive ailments, headaches or back pain which they never address. You may notice that they are not looking well or appear exhausted but they seem unaware. And they may talk in ways that signal they have little connection with others, inside or outside of work.

In the pre-burnout state, when the individual is driven by their need to achieve at any cost, they ignore what is happening to them but their brain does not. The sympathetic nervous system exists to stimulate the fight or flight response and to maintain the stability of our body as a system. When it reads an individual as being in a flight or fight situation, it prepares the body for dealing with that stress by increasing heart rate, increasing blood flow to the muscles, and closing down the digestive system.

The hypothalamic-pituitary-adrenal (HPA) axis then kicks in. Stress activates the hypothalamus, which in turn signals the pituitary to release the hormone ACTH to the adrenal glands. The adrenal glands, sitting on top of the kidneys, recognize the stress signal and respond by releasing cortisol and adrenaline. Cortisol and adrenaline are designed to support us through short periods of stress, just as they were designed to help us get out of the way of danger, or to fight at an earlier stage of our evolution. The adrenal glands are not designed for helping us respond to stress hour after hour, day after day. They get tired, and the weakening of the adrenal glands manifests as fatigue, lowered immune functioning, low mental energy, lowered blood pressure, and often cravings for salt and sugar. Over time, it is not just the body that begins to not function well. As mental effectiveness is reduced, the individual becomes trapped in a cycle of ever more effort with diminishing results. Eventually 'burnout' outs itself in a physical collapse, which causes an enforced break. The question then arises as to whether coaches can help clients reduce the heat before the point of collapse, or work with them to build a different way of working after collapse.

Since coaching is often offered to ambitious high achievers, it is helpful for the coach to be aware of the features of burnout, in order that they can challenge behaviours that the client will have come to view as 'normal'.

The following questions are those that I use with clients to help me understand their burnout risk:

- Have you noticed any changes in how you are thinking about yourself and your work?
- How would you describe your way of working?
- How would others describe your way of working?
- What are you not doing because of work?
- What are the costs of your commitment to work?
- What is it that makes work important to you?
- How well is that need being met?
- How would you describe your energy levels?
- Have you noticed any changes in your energy levels?
- What do you do when you are feeling tired?
- Are you experiencing any health issues?
- What have you done to deal with those health issues?
- Who do you seek support from?
- How do you look after yourself?
- What do you do after work/at the weekend that is unconnected to work?
- How do you switch off from work?
- If you were looking at your approach to work as an outsider, what would you see?
- What advice would you give yourself that you don't follow?
- What stops you?

Based on a client's answers to these questions, you can build a picture of whether the tiredness and overworking are a temporary response to an immediate need, or indicative of a person at risk. It also allows you to provide feedback based on your experience of other clients as to how 'normal' their way of working is, and the risks you see of their continuing with this approach. This does not guarantee that the client will accept your feedback, but it offers an opening for you to provide a reality check.

A vigilant coach can identify the warning signs of burnout and, with a duty of care, bring them to the attention of the client. You may be able to use the approaches described in the rest of this book to help the client build protection to prevent collapse. Alternatively, you may use the trust you have built to help the client seek specialist help.

Burnout is distinct from loss of resilience. An individual who is burnt out needs a period of recuperation while their body recovers from the stress they have placed it under, so it can return to a stable state. Only when they are stronger, and their adrenal glands replenished, will they be open to considering what they have learnt from the experience, and its meaning for their future working life. In contrast, loss of resilience is loss of access to a particular resource, in reaction to a particular event or a period of pressure. Whereas individuals who burn out create the conditions in which their individual needs and the environment they have chosen conflagrate, the same is not true of those who lose resilience – they react to what has happened to them, not to what they have created.

Summary

This chapter has been positioned to deepen your understanding of resilience by looking at:

- What resilience is and how we can understand it as a combination of genetics, the availability of protective factors, and learning.
- The importance of identity as a key variable in whether we are resilient or not in the face of a life disruption.
- How most resilience research is not based on individuals in work settings, and that recent work on adults and high achievers reinforces many of the themes of earlier research on children and adds new perspectives.
- Career resilience as a particular aspect of resilience that mainly focuses on the building of protection through action, rather than the building of internal capacity.
- The differences between resilience, PTSD, and burnout.

With that understanding of resilience, Chapter 2 invites you to consider how resilience has played out in your own life and how your learning can be of value when working with your clients.

2   You and your resilience

As a coach, you cannot work with clients at a level beyond which you would be willing to go. Asking a client to explore an issue at a level deeper than you would go, or to bring into the open a vulnerability that you would shy away from, is unethical. It moves you out of the space of partnering into positioning yourself as the doctor who can diagnose the condition, but does not want to experience it. Beyond issues of ethics, your ability to work with whatever your invitation opens up will be limited by your lack of consideration of yourself. Their disclosures may trigger issues within you that are unresolved. You will then be unavailable for your client, as your attention redirects itself to your inner dialogue and emotions.

Having addressed an issue, you will be more available and better equipped to work with it when a client brings it to you. It will open up your receptivity and creativity. Having worked through your issue, you will be able to access your insights in the service of your client's growth. It will support you in the dance of coaching because you will not just be following steps offered in a book, you will be able to improvise.

It was for this reason that when I began research on resilience, it was important that I looked at my own resilience, and that I understood how I had dealt with life difficulties. By doing so, I came to recognize what was different between the times when I remained resilient and those when I did not. I was able to identify what I could trust would still be accessible in tough times, and what is less available. I came to understand the model I had created, and what had shaped that model. I did this through talking with a psychotherapist who enabled me to understand the texture of my own resilience. This work has informed how I work with clients, and makes me more sensitive to the nuances of experience they bring to coaching.

I believe that just as I learnt a great deal through looking at my own resilience, the same will be true for you. That is why this chapter focuses on you. It is an invitation to take time out to consider your own experience, and to then draw out its value for working with others. It may prompt you to want to dig deeper by talking with a coach or psychotherapist. Even if it does not, working through this chapter will enhance your reading of the rest of the book.

Resilience Questionnaire

The Resilience Questionnaire is designed to help you assess the resilience qualities you possess as you live your daily life, so that you can recognize what enables you to be flexible in response to the demands of living and working. As you answer the questions, think of how you generally see yourself operating in the world. There are no right or wrong answers.

	Resilience Questionnaire					
		Strongly disagree				Strongly agree
	I have the ability to:	1	2	3	4	5
1.	Deal with the demands of my life					
2.	Be flexible in order to adapt to whatever I am presented with					
3.	Know what is important in my life					
4.	Change direction when the preferred route is not working					
5.	Ask for help when I need it					
6.	Find what I can take control of when things are uncertain					
7.	Control my emotions when feeling pressured					
8.	Face reality, even when it is difficult					
9.	Manage my way through difficulty					
10.	Focus on actions that move me towards longer term goals					
11.	Let go of what is not working					
12.	Recognize when others need support					
13.	Be decisive					
14.	Use strategies for managing my stress					
15.	Find solutions to the challenges I face					

16.	Recognize when I need to develop new behaviours and skills						
17.	Hold onto a sense of perspective even when things are difficult						
18.	Be proactive in addressing challenges						
19.	Remain optimistic even when things are tough						
20.	Acknowledge the difficulties of change and accept what has to be let go of						
21.	Be creative in finding ways of doing things even when resources are limited						
22.	Talk openly about frustrations with trusted colleagues, friends or family members						
23.	Deal with problems head-on, rather than hoping they will go away						
24.	Recognize when current pressures are affecting my responses						

Scoring the questionnaire

Transfer the scores you gave to each item on the Resilience Question-naire to the appropriate box below. Note the vertical listings of the statement numbers.

								Total
Self-belief	1		9		15			
Elasticity	2		16		20			
Meaning	3		10		17			
Solution finding	4		11		21			
Support	5		12		22			
Proactivity	6		13		18			
Emotional control	7		14		24			
Realistic positivity	8		19		23			

What does it tell you?

By looking at your profile, you will probably see that some qualities are more developed than others. Alternatively, you may see that you have a balanced profile in that all are present to a similar degree. If you find yourself with little differentiation, then ask yourself the question, 'which of these do I rely on most to get me through challenges?' Give those qualities an extra weighting.

How does your profile reflect how you present yourself to the world? Does it capture how you would describe yourself or how others signal that they see you?

The aim at this stage is to understand your starting place. The questionnaire is designed around eight contributors to resilience and its loss. These are based on recurring themes in resilience research.

Self-belief

The trust you have in your own actions and your capacity to deal with whatever comes your way.

Elasticity

The ability to adapt to changing circumstances and not stay attached to what is familiar and comforting.

Meaning

Having a sense of purpose and the creation of meaning helps people get through difficult times. It helps you know what you are working towards and why. Purpose helps us persist when things are difficult. Your meaning may come from attachment to a particular goal, or it may come from important values or beliefs that inform your life, such as religious faith or humanistic principles.

Solution finding

Being able to work with what is there and be creative in creating solutions, even when resources are limited or options narrow.

Support

What helps people through challenging times is the availability of emotional support, so that you know you are not facing things alone and are being listened to. It is equally important to be able to offer support to others, as it validates your worth.

Proactivity

Change and uncertainty can cause a freezing up, as individuals wait for ambiguity to disappear. Proactivity means taking action to improve the situation, rather than hoping things will get better or someone else will improve things for us.

Emotional control

When under pressure emotions become heightened and more volatile, with negative emotions often dominating how we assess the world and ourselves. Being able to manage our emotions helps us retain a sense of perspective, and to view problems at their correct size, rather than becoming overwhelmed by them.

Realistic positivity

Blind optimism has little value in getting us through difficulties because when expectations are not met, there is a collapse of belief and confidence. Realistic positivity comes from facing the reality of the situation, and assessing our strengths against that context. Being able to say, 'how can I make the best of what is happening right now?', rather than hoping things will just get better.

When your resilience is tested

The purpose of the questionnaire is to help you assess the benchmark position of your resilience in daily living. However, there is a difference between resilience viewed as a set of fixed qualities and resiliency. Resiliency is you in action. Eleanor Roosevelt allegedly said, 'People are like teabags, they don't know how strong they are until they are put in hot water.' Dipped in hot water, some people unearth qualities they did not know they had, while others find they are not as resourceful as they imagined.

In order for you to understand your resilience in action, it is useful to reflect on how you have reacted when facing a significant life difficulty.

When the going got tough

Think about a time when you faced a challenge, such as the loss of a job, the ending of a significant relationship, the death of someone close to you, infertility, illness or a severe downturn in your business. The experience should be one that falls into the category of normal life challenges, as distinct from the abnormal traumatic events that characterize post-traumatic stress syndrome.

Identify one situation where you coped well, perhaps better than you would have imagined. Identify a second situation where you did not cope so well. You may even have been surprised by how you responded. The event may not have been major and yet it had a profound effect on you. Take some time to write about the experiences under the headings given below.

Example 1: Where I remained resilient

The situation

The context in which it occurred

The resilience qualities I was able to access (use the Resilience Questionnaire as a reference point)

Other qualities or skills that helped me get through that are not represented in the questionnaire

What made it possible for me to access those qualities?

How they were of value to me

What they enabled me to do

Example 2: Where I lost access to my resilience

The situation.

The context in which it occurred

The resilience qualities I was not able to access (see Resilience Questionnaire)

Other qualities/skills I lost access to

What prevented me being able to access those qualities?

The consequences for how I dealt with the event

Reflective comparison

Based on what you have written about your two experiences, consider the different 'you' that you brought to each of them.

How would you see yourself in the first example?

- What image of yourself comes to mind?
- What words capture how you were at that time?
- What identity were you carrying with you?

When one client talked about a time when he was resilient, the image that came to his mind was of a tree standing in a field while a storm blew around it. The tree creaked at times, but stood firm. The words he used were *resolute, shaken at the edges but firm at the core*, and he was certain that eventually the storm would blow over. The identity that he carried with him was that of a survivor.

How would you see yourself in the second example?

- What image of yourself comes to mind?
- What words capture how you were at that time?
- What identity were you not able to access and what took its place?

The same client when he recalled a time when his resilience left him held an image of himself curled up in a corner with his hands over his head. The words he used to describe himself were *childlike, afraid, wanting to be rescued.* The identity he held was that of a victim.

When you compare your contrasting resilience experiences, what does that highlight for you? What does it add to your understanding of your own resilience?

Resilience in coaching

The previous section asked you to look at the big challenges you have faced, but the truth is that every coaching relationship tests our resilience. For example, you spend time planning for a session and the client takes the session in a completely different direction. A coaching relationship that had been going well suddenly derails, and the client signals a loss of confidence in your abilities. Your client is not taking the actions that they committed to and signals resistance to being pushed to explore the reality of what is stopping them. You get a less than positive evaluation at the end of the coaching relationship, which you thought had gone well. At such times, we have to draw on our resilience.

Accessing our resilience in the moment when coaching means being able to say, 'I don't feel this conversation is going well, what would be more helpful right now?' When you do so, you call on your self-belief. Being willing to let go of an expected direction in the conversation and follow the client shows that you have elasticity. Not relying on your toolkit of resources and inventing something in the moment calls on your solution building. Taking the risk of asking for client feedback on what you could do differently to help them requires an openness to asking for support. Taking the risk of challenging a client on their behaviour requires you to hold a sense of purpose. Noticing and then quietening your sense of panic when you feel the session slipping away requires that you can manage your emotions. Accepting what the client can do, rather than being disappointed because they do not do more, shows that you work with realistic positivity.

Reflect on your coaching

Think about coaching relationships that have not gone as well as you would have liked and consider them from the perspective of your resilience. What part did you play in the process? Did you lose purpose and focus, so that you and the sessions became directionless? Did the resistance of the client cause you to lose confidence in your own abilities? Did you find the client so challenging that your brain froze, or you were focused on your own emotions? Did you cling to an approach even if it was not successful because you could not think what else to do?

We have all had coaching relationships that tested our resilience. I once worked with a client who was a figure of fear for his staff – in fact, that was the reason for being asked to coach him. I noticed that before each session I became anxious that I would not be able to hold my standing with him. He was highly critical, and demanded I constantly explain what I was doing and why. I knew that if I did not hold the resilient me, I would fail him and myself. It was only when I accessed my sense of self-belief – the knowledge that I am a skilled coach, and reminded myself of that fact in the ladies before each meeting – that I was able to become an equal partner with him. When I walked through the door with that knowledge, I was able to use his criticism of me as a useful tool to feed back to him the impact he had on others when he challenged them.

Now consider a coaching relationship that went well but was challenging. You may have liked the client, or it may have been the sort of issue you enjoy working with, but the work was not easy. On reflection, which aspects of your resilience were you able to access? For example, you discovered that you were willing to let go of structure, because you had a sense of trust that you would deal with whatever emerged. Or, you stuck with the uncomfortable parts of the relationship because you had a clear sense of purpose in what you were bringing to the interactions. Or, you were able to offer strong challenge, because even if the client pushed back, you were confident in your ability to deal with their emotions.

One of my clients was seen as brilliant but tricky. She was a creative workaholic who could outthink her colleagues, and appeared to need little sleep. She would send emails in the middle of the night, and would be the only person in a senior management meeting to have read every document, no matter how hefty. She made those around her feel permanently on the back foot. She talked constantly with hardly a space for breath. She was also extremely engaging. It was easy as a coach to be swept along in the enjoyment of listening to her, without adding anything to her thinking. Being resilient in working with her meant not being caught up in the need to look clever, but rather being clear that it was my role to be firm in stopping her talking, and to enable her to start noticing herself and the impact of her style. It meant holding onto a sense of purpose, as she was explaining away with brilliant rationale her behaviours.

Taking your learning back into resilience coaching

From looking at your own resilience when tested, you will have insights that you can take into your work. It will have helped you to identify what you need to be alert to in yourself, so that you remain resilient in the moment within a coaching session. It will have helped you better understand your resilience qualities and the model you have created about what stays with you and what becomes more difficult to access when under stress. You can use your understanding of yourself to help your client better understand their own resilience, its strengths and its gaps.

Summary

This chapter has invited you to examine your own experience by:

- Assessing your resilience as it operates on a daily basis using a resilience questionnaire based on a mix of trait and protective factors identified from research.
- Offering you a questionnaire to use with your clients to help them understand their own resilience profile.
- Deepening understanding of your resilience in action by writing about two contrasting experiences and noticing differences in your response.
- Looking at your resilience within coaching sessions.
- Encouraging you to reflect on the meaning of your own experience for how you work with your clients.
- Providing you with exercises to use with clients to help them recognize that resilience is not a have or have not quality, and to support understanding of their own response patterns.

3   The loss of resilience narrative

The man in front of me had lost his job. He was experienced, highly qualified and marketable, yet he found it impossible to take action. Although visibly anxious, he did not raise his concerns with his family, because he did not want them to feel that their lives would be changed in any way by his 'failure'. His reactions were partly shaped by his social context, which told him he should ensure a solid middle-class life for his children. They were also partly shaped by the conditioning of his formative years, which told him that as a man he was the main provider, and that choosing a profession guaranteed stability. It was further shaped by a personality that valued security, and an identity that was strongly connected to his status within work. When identities that were important to his sense of self were challenged by redundancy, he became caught in the shadows of those identities. The stable provider became the failed caretaker and the skilled professional became the unemployable reject. Until he was able to recognize the narrative he had built, and how it limited his choices, it was impossible for him to act.

'A man is a teller of tales, he lives surrounded by his stories... he sees everything that happens to him through them, and he tries to live his own life, as if he were telling a story.' Jean Paul Sartre's observation on the importance of our own stories as shapers of our lives is lived out every day in coaching sessions. A new client sends us their CV to show how they present themselves to the world. It is their public story. Alongside the public story, the client holds hidden stories of who they are, what they can achieve, what they should expect, and what is allowable for them. They carry the unspoken stories with them into every situation they face. Those stories signal how they want to be seen: hardworking or naturally gifted, a tiger parent or a relaxed one, ambitious or just lucky. These stories are constructions. They are selective. They do not hold absolute truths. They are acts of interpretation, but they allow the client to manage what they show to the world. They help sustain an identity. For as long as the story follows the narrative line that has been created, an individual is unlikely to seek our help. But then, something changes: either the old story no longer works, or the story is disrupted by an event that challenges their view of themselves. It is then that narrative becomes an area of focus.

Story-telling

Fairy stories have a beginning, a middle marked by difficulty, and a happy ending. As children we love the certainty that after danger or difficulty a certain future is established. Classic stories have a more complex arc. They begin with a life being lived in a predictable way, which is followed by a trigger: something that is beyond the control of the protagonist. That trigger leads to a quest where the main character looks to find a way back to certainty. It is seen in clients who are desperate to find a new partner immediately after the end of a relationship, to be back on the talent grid after the failure of a project, or to find a replica of the job they have just lost. In the middle of the story, obstacles and complications thwart the quest. Getting back to what was before proves difficult, and it leads to the point where the character has to make a critical choice. They are confronted by a decision: a choice of paths, from which the rest of the story will follow. It shows up in clients who are faced with the decision to continue trying to strive for the top or to live a more balanced life; whether to follow their values or their material desires; whether to give up on a relationship or accept the limitations of what is possible. Once the decision is made, the character will act on the choice, and the story moves towards a resolution in which the main character is revealed as being changed by the experience, and a new 'normal' begins. Clients do not usually seek coaches when the storyline is working; they find us when the quest is proving difficult. They are stuck in the middle of their story unable to make a critical choice. They may come with the expectation that their work with us will enable them to restore what was, or they may come with the knowledge that the existing story has run its course, but they cannot see what the next chapter is. In both cases, our role is in helping them to understand the narrative they bring and to support them in creating a new one.

In this chapter, the focus is on how to help clients both create written accounts of their experience and enable them to tell their story. It is through this dual process that the client can reveal the identity that has been threatened by a difficult experience. In the following chapter, the focus will be on the role of the coach in helping clients to find alternative identities from which a new narrative can be built.

The link between resilience and written narrative

The link between resilience and written narrative has been made per-suasively by the social psychologist James Pennebaker, whose work on the relationship between language and recovery from trauma has dem-onstrated that asking clients to write about events that have emotional meaning strengthens their immune system: they literally become stronger. Writing as a form of confession reduces the stress on the body, which in turn speeds up the healing process. Writing during challenging times helps provide protection against psychosomatic disorders, and those who write about their difficulties make less use of medical services. What is key in the writing is that the individual is able to express the emotions attached to the event, and does not simply recount the 'story'.

Authors will often claim that writing about a significant life event has been cathartic: they literally feel better as a result of putting it down in writing. That feeling may reflect shifts at an immune system level, but Pennebaker argues it is also because the process of writing helps cogni-tive processing. It allows the person to transform a painful personal mem-ory that is being experienced at a sensory level within the body into an organized linguistic form. Powerful evidence of this was found in a study that offered unemployed adults the opportunity to write about their feel-ings and thoughts in response to unemployment. Those who wrote were so much more successful in finding work than the control group, that the study was halted on the grounds that the study was unfair to those not writing. It was not that writing led participants to undertake more job search than the control group. In fact, there was little difference between the two in the amount of job search activity. It was that writing allowed for the reframing of thoughts and feelings about their situation, so that they went out into the job market carrying a narrative that better sup-ported their job search.

Jennifer Pals, a researcher on writing as therapy, argues that there is a three-stage process of recovery. In stage 1, writing is a means of acknow-ledging the impact of the event. In stage 2, the author examines the narra-tive they have created, and from this comes stage 3 when the narrative is transformed. Coaches have a role at each stage of this process.

Writing in the moment

A further piece of evidence on the value of writing comes from the analysis by Joshua Smyth of existing research on written narrative. From his meta-analysis, he concluded that it was important that the individual is writing about a current rather than a past event, and that the writing is spaced over time. Asking a client to write about something that happened some time before does not have the same power, because they have already rewritten their account. It is why autobiographies can never be truthful. By the time the book is written, the author knows the outcome of the critical event, and the account is written with that knowledge. It enables them to claim that facing addiction, coming out or losing their position as CEO was the best thing that could have happened to them. They can claim this because they now know what it led to. Had they written their account while living in the middle of the process, it would have been written very differently. It is when the client is in the middle of difficulty that writing has its greatest power. Test this premise for yourself.

Think of an event that has been significant for you, because it was a break in how you expected your life to operate. From where you stand now, how would you write about that experience? What have you learnt from that experience that has been of value to you in how you live your life? Now journey back to the middle of that experience. How would you be writing about that event then? What would that version tell you about the person you were, and what you needed to learn?

Writing about an event once has less value than writing repeatedly. Repeated writing is important because it enables the author to notice changes in themselves, and to be aware that their feelings and thoughts change continuously. It allows the writer to recognize that although times are tough, there will be times when things are better, and to interrogate what influences those feelings. It enables them to notice how their language changes as their relationship with the event changes. The length of the writing is less important than having multiple opportunities to reflect and to track shifts in thinking. Writing creates space. In creating that space, it allows the client to move from being caught in the story to a position where they can look at themselves as an object of enquiry.

Narrative and identity

When writing a novel, the author controls the identity they wish us as readers to attach to the characters: the good man or the bad, the victim or the champion over adversity, the winner or the disappointed. Living our own story, that clarity of identity can be hidden from us, but when we write an account of any key event in our life, our 'truth' will be shaped by the identity that we attach to our telling. The very structure of a story invites us to place ourselves as a clearly defined character within that account. As a coach helping a client to unearth the identity they are carrying, is the starting point for enabling them to examine the value of that identity in relationship to their desire for change.

When a client comes to us because their resilience has been impacted, they are carrying a story with a title: the end of my career dream, the failure of leadership, prejudice trumps ability. Within that story, the author attributes him or herself an identity: martyr, victim, loser, whistle-blower or betrayed. The identity they bring is one that is a consequence of the loss of access to an identity they value. Each of us has identities that sustain us in our sense of self in the world. For many executive coaching clients, it is linked to an identity they have created for themselves within work. Sometimes that identity seems obvious. Someone who has reached a senior level is likely to hold identities linked to success, winning, strength, ability, and power. They may also hold less obvious identities linked to being wanted, valued, respected or feared. Similarly, those dealing with life coaching issues may be working with a client whose identity of good wife, guiding parent, healthy adult or autonomous child has been challenged by an event that revealed such identities are not fixed. In their place they bring to coaching identities related to their unloveability, failure to protect, age or vulnerability.

In the midst of pain, a client can lose access not just to a sustaining identity, but also to the truth that they hold multiple identities. The martyr presented in the telling of a client's story can be the assertive protagonist in another context. Images of self are shaped by context, and those images are as much shaped by the social constraints that individuals place on themselves as what is allowable. A client who tells of fighting for the rights of their disabled child may present themselves as powerless when fighting for their own rights within a work team. Focusing on understanding identity within a particular event enables the coach to recognize what in the client's stable sense of self has been breached, and what they have replaced it with. The quest then shifts from trying to reinstate the old story, which is often the client's hope, to how to enable the client to find alternative identities from which a new narrative can emerge.

Case study: Unearthing the identity

Jan had worked for her organization for many years and had reached a senior role. Her career had been shaped by what her bosses told her was in her best interests, and she had accepted their directions and shown commitment and loyalty. She believed that by doing what was expected of her she would be valued and taken care of. Her sustaining identity was that of the valued retainer. When asked to apply for a role during restructuring, she was devastated when she wasn't even shortlisted. She could not believe that her boss could reward her loyalty with disloyalty. Her narrative about herself had been disrupted, since her boss's decision showed she had no value. When asked to write about the event, she positioned herself as the loyal servant who had been betrayed. Her account was that of a powerless victim. As a senior manager, she would never have described herself in those terms, but when she wrote her story, it became clear that she was creating a future based on being that powerless victim. It was self-evident that this identity was of no value to her in taking control over her future, and that the work of coaching was in helping her access other identities which would enable her to regain control.

Structuring a narrative

Because I enjoy writing, I have often erroneously believed that clients also do. Experience has taught me that many clients associate writing with painful educational experiences. Equally, just because a client is an elegant drafter of policy documents, it does not translate into being comfortable when writing about him or herself. Many a journal I have handed out at the beginning of a coaching relationship has never appeared at any subsequent session. Therefore, when I became interested in using narrative within my research on resilience coaching, I realized that unstructured journaling was unlikely to be of use to clients. I decided instead to create a structure within which clients could write, that would allow them to give an account of the event, but which would also encourage them to explore context, their feelings and thoughts about the event, and the understanding they have taken from it. What ending had they already created that limited their view of the future?

The following structure can be used to begin the work of identifying what in a client's resilience has been impacted, and the identity they are bringing to their narrative creation.

Exercise 3.1

Invite your client to write about the incident that they have identified as impacting on them. Encourage them to be free in how they write, and not to be concerned about their grammar or spelling. It is not a test of their skills in literature or language. It is the chance to put down on paper thoughts that they carry about the event. It is their private story.

Ensure they do not see it as essay writing. There is no right length.

1. What has happened?
2. When did it happen?
3. Who is involved?

4. What is the context in which it has happened?
5. How do you understand the event – what realization or learning has it given you?
6. What thoughts do you have in relation to what has happened?
7. What effect is it having on you – what are you noticing about yourself (even if others are not noticing)?
8. How do you see your future right now?

The purpose of the written narrative is to help the identification of the coaching focus. I offer it to clients as the basis for a first coaching session, once it has been agreed that we will work together. The purpose in offering it before the first session is that it allows for the first session to focus on expanding the story in their telling of it, and to inform agreement on the focus of the coaching.

Before using this with a client, apply it to yourself. Focus on a current difficulty. It does not need to be a major problem, just something that is preying on your mind. You may have not been selected as a coach when you thought you had established a strong connection in the 'chemistry meeting' and it was an organization you really wanted to work with. You may have failed to win a tender in which you had invested a lot of effort. Write your account of it as you are experiencing it today, using the narrative questions, without censoring your thoughts and feelings. Then read the account as though you were outside of the event. What does this story tell you about the author: what beliefs or assumptions reside within this account? What does the language of the account suggest about how the author sees him or herself? Are there clues as to an identity that has been challenged by this event? What in this account is unhelpful to the author? If you were coaching this person, what would you be interested in exploring with them?

The value of repeated writing

In asking a client to write an initial account, it allows for the writing of a last account before the final coaching session – as a means of recognizing the extent to which their narrative has been rewritten.

In the final account, the client is invited to address the following questions:

1. What are your thoughts now about your future?
2. What if anything has changed for you?
3. How do you now understand the event that happened to you – what realization or learning has it given you?

4. What thoughts do you now have about yourself in relation to what happened?
5. What feelings do you now have in relation to what happened?
6. What are you now noticing about yourself?
7. What insights will you be able to draw on in the future to help you deal with future challenges?

The purpose of the final account is to enable the client to recognize the shift in their narrative, and their identity within it, and to look at learning in terms of their future. It is important that they see the value of their new narrative and its place in dealing with future challenges, rather than just in the context of the issue that brought them to you. What have they learnt that they now take with them to support them in facing their next challenge? It is an acknowledgement that protection from difficulty is not possible, but their own resilience skills can better prepare them for how they handle the next challenge.

Case study: The second narrative

When Jan came for coaching, her expectation was that the work would focus on how to make her boss recognize his unfairness, so that he would value her, and a new opportunity would be created. She brought the hope that somehow she could change his decision if she behaved differently. Over the course of the coaching, she came to recognize that the powerless victim did not serve her well, and it did not reflect the other identities she had available to her. The coaching unearthed an identity she did not realize she had: the acceptor of uncertainty. She had spent so much of her life with one organization and looking to create security within it, that she assumed that that was what she had to have in order to be resilient. However, when she looked to events in her personal life, she recognized that she had managed her way through significant life difficulties by tolerating uncertainty. By the end of the coaching, her immediate situation looked no different. She still did not have a new role, but she had decoupled herself from her future being based on her boss's largesse. She no longer talked in the language of victim, and she trusted that an identity of being tolerant of uncertainty would serve her better. Her future was one of positive emergence.

Intermediate writing

Research has shown that it is regularity of writing that makes a difference. A paragraph once a week is of more value than a one-off lengthy piece because regularity of writing allows changes in perception, nuance, and language to be noticed. Reflecting regularly keeps the client engaged in the work of creating a new narrative. Some clients respond readily to the idea of taking ten minutes once a week to write about how they are now feeling and thinking in relationship to the focus of coaching. Others struggle, or even resist. While every exercise we offer to clients is an invitation rather than a directive, I have discovered that where the client sees that their writing is valued, and used within coaching sessions to inform the focus of the conversation and to recognize progress, they are more likely to engage. When they see the writing as a reflection of where they are in their coaching journey, rather than a task set by the coach, their relationship with the idea of writing can shift.

The two narratives

There are two forms of narrative: what we write and what we speak. Within coaching they have distinct purposes. While writing in itself helps the regaining of resilience, there is a distinct value in the telling of a story. Individuals understand themselves through the language they use, and the language they use in telling their story to another person is different from that used in writing. When clients write an account, they are selective and look to work within the strictures of story-telling. Characters are clearly defined. There is a desire to create a coherent whole, and to edit out aspects that might blur that coherence. That is helpful in sharpening understanding of issues of challenged identity. However, the telling of a story adds a key dimension: the availability of an audience. You as the coach are that audience. The quality of your listening enables the story to be expanded and deepened. Children often ask of carers that they create stories. If the story is one that engages them, they will look to the story-teller to develop the story, to tell more. The knowledge of the child's investment in the story leads the teller into expanding the detail, and extending the plot, often into areas they would never have imagined. A story which if written would have moved quickly from 'once upon a time' to 'happily ever after' becomes more complex with each telling, because of the attention of the listener. The coach is often the first audience for a story that hitherto has existed only in the client's head. The invitation to 'tell me more' enables the client to go beyond the written account. The coach listens for what the client wants to achieve in telling the story in a particular way and for what their narrative line is omitting. They look for what the client is projecting onto others, and the beliefs that underpin their account. The coach asks questions. In their questioning they become co-author of the story, and a different version emerges. The story is changed by the attentiveness of the coach. Narrative coach David Drake talks of the creation of a 'third space' when narrative is brought into coaching. The account of the story-teller and the attention of the skilled listener create an alchemy from which something entirely new is created. It is in that space that the work of the coaching is defined, and the work of coaching the narrative operates. The coach is not just a passive audience. They are able to feedback what they hear in the story, to explore the impact of that narrative on how the client is living their life, and to unearth what aspects of their resilience have been impacted by the event.

Working with their narrative

After the client has written their account, invite them to send it to you in advance of the session, if they are comfortable doing so. The purpose of this is for the coach to gain a first sense of what is revealed in their language and how they write about themselves. If the client prefers not to, then the exercise can be adapted, so that the written account is read after the client has told their story. This reversal allows the coach and coachee to note changes between the written and spoken versions.

Thank your client for having written their account, and ask for any thoughts that emanated from their writing. Explain that because we write differently from how we speak, it can be helpful to tell a story, because there is then an audience who can ask questions, which will add to understanding.

Position yourself as passionately wanting to understand their story, and thus with their permission you would like to ask questions as they speak, and to occasionally write down something which strikes you when listening to them. You will share those thoughts later on.

Invite your client to put aside their written account to tell their story in their own voice. As you listen to them, listen in particular to repeated words, or clusters of words that point to an important idea or feeling that is associated with their story. Note down those words.

Once they have finished their account, invite them to reflect on what they have heard in listening to themselves. Then ask if they would be open to you feeding into the conversation those things that you were struck by when listening to them. You could reflect back the feelings that the story has evoked in you, to determine whether they reflect their own feelings. You may want to check on beliefs or values that you experienced as underpinning how they related their story. You can test out words you were struck by when listening to their account, and invite them to consider if they see any patterns. Your clustering of words around key themes can be powerful in revealing to the client the identity that is shaping their narrative, and help them direct the focus of their work onto re-finding their resilient self.

Case study: Hearing the narrative

When Jan brought her narrative to the coaching session, she wanted to read it out, as though she was reporting to her teacher. I stopped her and asked her to put the paper down, and to tell me what had happened in her own voice. I asked if it would be acceptable if I wrote down things that struck me as significant as she spoke. She agreed. As she told her account, there were some similarities with the written version, but in listening to her, her voice and the language she used became more emotional. The author of the written account had controlled her voice in order that her account of unfairness would seem reasonable. When she told her story, it was full of anger and fear. As I reflected back what I was hearing, she was able to expose more of what she was feeling. She was able to let out the internal voice that was telling her she was not worth caring for, that she had been stupid to believe that loyalty counted for anything, and that she was too old to expect anything different. In hearing back her own language she recognized that it revealed truths that she had not felt safe in admitting in her written account. Hearing her words expressed by another, she was able to identify that her moving on required her to re-find her confidence, and to move from being dependent on others to being an autonomous adult.

We live by the stories we create. Our role as coaches is to help our clients recognize the story they carry when dealing with difficulty so that they can, like a Hollywood film director, decide if the story works. Many a successful film had to be reshot after preview reaction indicated that it did not work. There is no one ending. It is about helping the client to create the one that best serves their purpose. Often our clients bring their stories without being conscious that they can shoot alternative versions. They believe they have acted in the only way they can. It is in the writing and telling of their story that coaches can make them aware of their own assumptions, and in particular how they are limiting their possibilities by being attached to an identity that does not serve them well in managing their way through a difficulty. Recognizing that their story is only a partial account of who they are provides a starting point for the work of coaching.

Having enabled your client to share their narrative, the focus shifts to how you as a coach can enable the process of building a new narrative, and in particular to understanding the process by which a new narrative emerges.

Summary

This chapter has explored the value of working with narrative by:

- Establishing strong research evidence for the value of working with clients' writing when dealing with issues that test their resilience.
- Offering a structure for repeated writings about a key event.
- Separating out the distinctive value of written and spoken narrative in working with clients.
- Positioning identity as a key factor in explaining why resilience has been lost, and the importance of accessing alternate identities as central to recovery and moving forward with learning.

4   Coaching the narrative

Listening to the narrative that your client brings is central to understanding what in their resilience has been impacted. At this point you are probably asking, 'So now I understand what is holding my client back, how do I help them build capability or re-find their resilience?' You want to get into the work of coaching. The remainder of the book will enable you to do so, by offering you a range of choices for how you address the issues unearthed by the narrative. This chapter is a gateway to you making the right choice because it focuses on the process by which a narrative gets changed, and the challenges faced by our clients in being able to do so.

When my son was young, he demanded that a particular story be read to him every night. It was called 'Owl Babies', and it told the story of three young owls who were cared for by their loving mother. Each night she went out to find food for them, but one night she did not return. The owlets became increasingly anxious. The older ones tried to find explanations for her absence, but the youngest one just cried repeatedly. Eventually the mother owl returned. Seeing the impact her absence had had, she reassured them that she would always come back, and the baby owl cried out in joy, 'I love my Mummy'. At first this story of love and reassurance had to be read nightly, then it was interspersed with other stories, until finally it was dismissed as babyish and never asked for again. Its purpose had been served. My son had absorbed that he could trust that his mother would always be there to give him love and care, even if not physically present. Once he had that knowledge, he no longer needed that story.

Our clients are no different from my son. They have stories that they hold onto. They are stories about themselves in the world. The difference between a child and an adult is that the child recognizes more easily when the story has served its purpose and can be let go of, as they move onto their next stage of development. As adults we often carry old stories, or ones that limit our actions, and it is within coaching that the limits of stories can be recognized and new ones constructed. The work is in helping clients build an alternative narrative that will better support their resilience, while acknowledging that changing a story is not easy.

When talking with groups, I sometimes show a picture by Vermeer entitled, 'Lady writing a letter with her maid'. It shows a woman bent over a desk writing a letter, while her maid looks out of the window, holding a blue handkerchief over her stomach. Google it, so you can share in this exercise. I then ask the participants to tell me the story of this picture. In a room of thirty individuals, there will be thirty different interpretations. Some people see the maid as a courier for a love letter, others that the maid is pregnant and the letter is one of dismissal, yet others that she is simply bored with the demands of her job and is desperate to get out into the streets below. Whatever story they create, I then ask them to accept the version of another person. There is an immediate resistance. Already they have become attached to their story as holding the truth. It is cleverer, subtler, more accurate, more psychologically complex than the other person's interpretation. That is how it is with the stories our clients bring to us. They are strongly attached to them, even though other versions are available.

Immunity to change

If we are going to help our clients change their narrative, it is important that we acknowledge just how strongly attached they are to the one they bring. Robert Kegan and Lisa Lahey of Harvard Business School have spent thirty years studying people who are wanting to effect change, and have concluded that no matter how much a person wants to make a change, there are hidden motivations and beliefs that prevent them doing so. They call this phenomenon 'immunity to change'. It is why people fail to make lifestyle changes even when their health is in danger, or don't act on those things that they claimed with confidence they were going to do within a coaching session. The psychologist William Perry presents it as the challenge of understanding both what a client really wants and what they will do to avoid getting it.

The difficulty of change should not be underestimated. It is no longer possible for clients to claim that 'an old dog can't be taught new tricks'. Neuroscience has taken away that defence, with its discovery of the neuroplasticity of the brain. The removal of the age barrier to learning means understanding what is keeping the client from changing their story becomes even more important. From another perspective, Kegan and Lahey in repeatedly interviewing participants over many years discovered that adults' ability to deal with mental complexity does not plateau once adulthood is reached, as earlier researchers on adult development had argued. Rather, over a lifetime, the ability to deal with complexity follows a slight upward curve. It is an undulation, rather than a straight line. There are times of change and times of stability. There are times when an individual wants to hold onto what they know and believe, and times when they are able to expand what they know and believe. The skill of a coach is in being able to find ways of enabling the client to be open to that expansion, by recognizing where the immunity to change lies, and then supporting the client in strengthening their immune system, so that it is stronger and able to accommodate greater complexity. It is in holding that complexity that an alternative story can develop.

The Narrative Wave™

The question of how a story is changed is one that I brought to my own research. I wanted to understand how coaching could help participants tell their story. I wanted to understand how a story changes, but also what role the coach plays in that process. I did not focus on any one technique, since as the rest of this book argues there are many ways by which resilience issues can be addressed within coaching. I was interested in the part the coach plays in strengthening a client's immune system, so that a new narrative can be allowed in. I did this through recording and then analysing in detail coaching sessions conducted with research participants. I was looking for differences that emerged from session to session. It enabled me to understand the extent to which constructs were carried from one session to the next or were let go of. It made me aware of new ideas brought into a session as a signal of shift, and those ideas brought in to halt the narrative changing.

The picture that emerged was not one of steady progress, whereby each session built on the learning of the last, with constant movement towards an end goal. The picture was that of a wave, as shown in Figure 4.1.

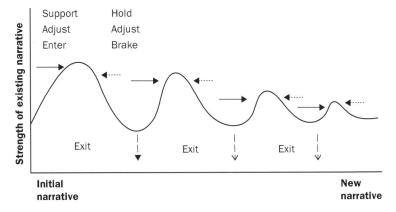

Figure 4.1 The Narrative Wave™

When clients come to coaching, they are holding a story. The story may not be of value to them in moving forward, but it keeps them afloat. Within coaching, the experience of sharing their narrative makes clear to them that need to do more than float – they need to be able to swim towards the shore. The shore is visible in the goals they have set themselves, but in getting there, it is as if they are a swimmer who has become caught in a cross current. As fast as they progress towards a new narrative, they are also knocked off course. This shows itself in the themes revealed in the analysis of coaching sessions:

- *Holding*: Themes related to the loss of resilience carried from one coaching conversation to the next.
- *Supporting*: Positive themes carried from a previous session into the next and providing support to the regaining of resilience.
- *Adjusting*: Themes that repeat an idea from a previous session, but take a different position in relation to it. The adjustment could be either supportive of or challenging to the regaining of resilience.
- *Exiting*: Themes from one session that do not reappear in any subsequent session.
- *Braking*: New themes that enter to slow or halt progress.
- *Entering*: New themes that usher in thoughts, feelings or behaviours that the client sees as supporting their resilience.

What the shape of The Narrative Wave™ shows is that the creation of a new narrative comes from allowing the client to find ways of negotiating the waters that hold their story. While heading towards shore, the client is constantly halted by a wave pushing them back or sideways. Movement forward through finding a new thought or feeling creates a backwash that allows brakes or adjustments. Slowly the movement towards the shore becomes steadier, but the end point is not calm water. It is enough that the waves have settled sufficiently for a new narrative to be accommodated. It does not ask that the old story disappear. It may still be a small surface wave, but its power has been sufficiently reduced that that it has a different place within a more complex story.

When this does not happen, and the client constantly brings in new brakes, refuses to let old ideas exit or negatively adjusts any new idea that emerges, The Narrative Wave™ can appear as in Figure 4.2. Here the client is trapped by their initial narrative. The effort needed to make any progress is enormous, because with each push forward there is a countervailing push back. The waters remain choppy and while the client obtains insight, the forces against using that insight use up so much energy that they are unable to strengthen their immune system sufficiently to accommodate a new story.

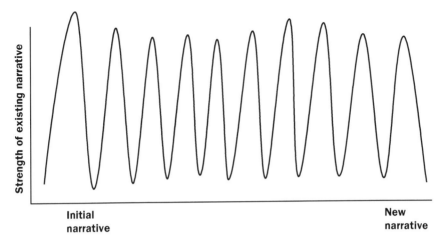

Figure 4.2   A holding wave pattern

How to recognize where a client is in their story

Once you accept that progress is not linear or cyclical with predictable stages of progression, you are then ready as a coach to start tracking your clients. You will be alert to what is carried from one session to another. You will recognize when a brake is being applied to a shift that you thought had been embedded. You will notice what has both entered and exited. This can be done by making narrative part of your reflection on each coaching session.

Ask yourself the following questions:

1. What thoughts or feelings from the previous session were repeated in this session?
2. What has exited? What was present in the previous session that did not have a place in this one?
3. What new ideas or feelings were introduced into this session which are helpful to their movement?
4. What brake to movement did they bring to the session?
5. What idea or feeling that was present in the last session was re-presented but with a different interpretation?

If you were going to draw your coaching relationship as a wave, what is the wave pattern?

By recognizing the wave pattern, you can prepare yourself for your next conversation. It helps you to recognize what is holding them back, as well as what is helping them to move forward, so that the brakes and negative adjustments can be looked at together. It also allows you to hold up a mirror to your client, so they can see where their thinking is already changing.

The role of the coach

Our task as coaches is to support clients in learning to swim more easily, so that a new narrative can emerge. It was for that reason that I analysed by own work as a coach. I was interested in what I did that impacted on why one client would make more progress than another. Where individuals with seemingly equally strong desires to move beyond their difficulty and to re-find their resilience had different outcomes, what might I be doing as a coach that supported or got in the way of their progress? By looking at what my intentions were in each intervention, rather than focusing on what techniques I used in any particular session, I was able to separate myself from trying to defend my skill as a coach and to look instead at the patterns of how I intervened. Those patterns emerged in a model of five key processes (Figure 4.3) for helping a client create a sustainable narrative. These patterns were found across the entire coaching relationship, and also within coaching sessions.

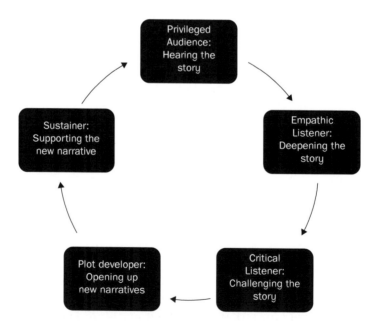

Figure 4.3   The coach in the resilience coaching process

At the beginning, the coach's role is to be the privileged audience, sig-nalling that they want to understand what the event means to the client, and its impact on them. As the narrator comes to trust in the coach's non-judgemental, fully engaged listening, rapport builds and the coach is able to start probing to help the client understand their own story at a deeper level. This probing is designed to allow them to own the identity that has been impacted, and the shadow identity that they have attached to them-selves in its place. That process can take more than one session, but it is central to the client being willing to start letting go of the shadow identity that they feel they have been fully heard. I discovered through analysing my own work that when I hurried the process, because of a desire to get on with the 'coaching', the client would keep going back over the same narrative. It is like a child who, when they cannot get their parent's full attention, simply repeats the same phrase until they know they have been heard. Before a client is willing to be open to challenging their own story and exploring what they may be attached to even if it makes no logical sense, they need to know that the coach 'gets' why this event is so impor-tant to them and their sense of self. Clients often want to offer far more detail than the coach sees as relevant, but it needs to be heard through the client's lens of what they are wanting to show by offering that level of detail.

Once the coach can hear that the client has reached a point where they are tired of telling their story and want to do something different, the coach has the invitation to become the critical listener. The client is now ready to be challenged, using the full repertoire of your coach-ing toolkit, to align with their need. The remaining chapters offer ideas on how this can be done from the perspectives of cognitive behavioural therapy, positive psychology, acceptance and commitment therapy, solu-tion-focused coaching, mindfulness, and career coaching. You may be strongly committed to one of the many other ways in which coaches can work with clients. The selection in this book is based on my own experi-ence and evidence from research in working with resilience issues. Any alternative approach you bring can work equally well, as long as it is positioned at the correct point in the coaching cycle, and your client has trust in your intent.

The purpose of challenging the story through bringing into play your coaching tools is to enable the client to start bringing in new thoughts and feelings, and to help them remove the brakes stopping them swimming faster. As the wave formation changes, the new nar-rative begins to build; your client allows in other identities that can be used to sit alongside and eventually dispel the shadow identity. It is from the process of profound listening and skilful challenging that the client is able to find a new narrative. The stage at which the new narrative emerges is an exciting one for the client and the coach. There is a shared pleasure in witnessing the client become more than they thought they were. They are energized, and self-belief returns. However, the work is not done at this point. The challenge is how to enable the client to sustain this narrative, so that it becomes a narrative in action, attached to the implementation of important goals, once you are no longer present.

Sustaining a narrative

Amy Brann, a coach and neuroscientist, tells us that within the brain there are billions of basal ganglia. The basal ganglia are responsible for storing routines, repetitive thoughts and behaviours. Information is relayed to the basal ganglia by two additional parts of the brain: the dorsolateral striatum and dorsomedial striatum. The dorsolateral striatum is associated with habits. It helps us perform the many habitual things we do each day, from brushing our teeth to remembering to switch off the lights before leaving the house. It also relays the repetitive thoughts each of us has, so that they are laid down in the brain. We are all creatures of habit, and the stories we hold are also habits. However, changing a story is not as simple as replacing one story with a newly written one. While the neural circuits attached to the old story may weaken, the story is still available. As illustrated in The Narrative Wave™, the old story can continue to have a place even though a new one has been formed. The story may appear to be out of print, but under stress individuals revert to their old habit. How many times have you found yourself when under stress going back to old ways of behaving and thinking, even though you know they are not good for you? What helps to intervene in that process is the dorsomedial striatum. It is associated with goal-directed actions. Whether it is eating healthier in order to lose weight before Christmas or running to become fit, our new habit is better sustained through attachment to a goal. What often throws us is the realization that even though we may have a very clear goal, we can still revert to the old story. That realization can cause clients to believe the new story is less true than the old story. That is why sustaining the new story is a key part of coaching a client back to resilience. It is common for the emergence of a new narrative to be quickly linked to a goal. The client will see claiming a more proactive self or accepting they can be confident as enablers of achieving whatever goal they wish to achieve. However, what they will be less aware of is the power of the old story. It is therefore central to coaching for resilience that the coach addresses the importance of sustainability.

Sustaining a story

When clients are excited by the possibilities that come with their new narrative, the coach's role becomes one of testing commitment, to unearth those things that could undermine them and drive them back to the comfort of the old story. Questions that can be useful at this stage include:

- What do you fear about acting on the new story? For example, not being liked, being put in the spotlight, discovering you can't…
- How real is that fear?
- How important is your goal in relation to that fear?
- What can you draw on to help reduce the fear?
- What are you committed to that competes with acting on the new story? For example, are you more committed to being seen as a nice person than being an ambitious person? Are you more committed to being below the radar than being in the spotlight? Are you more committed to safety than taking a risk?
- How willing are you to challenge the dominant commitment?
- If you have the will to challenge the dominant commitment, what would be a sign of that challenge?
- If you are not willing to challenge the commitment, what is still possible?
- What do you assume will happen if you act on the new story? For example, that your colleagues will not include you in social events. You will freeze in the spotlight. It will be the end of your career.
- What evidence do you have that your assumption is true?
- What would be a more useful assumption that would support you in acting on your new story?
- Even if the assumption is true, what are you still willing to do?

Case study: Sustaining a story

Francis had a story that he was a quiet reflector who could not impact on a highly extroverted, activist boss. Within weeks of being promoted, he was talking of leaving. He could not stand the competitive environment his boss had created within the team, with people expected to make instant decisions in order to impress rather than thinking things through. Francis was stressed and he was having difficulty sleeping. He came with a story of the powerlessness of the introvert, but over time he created a new story of the power of introversion and considered action. He came to see that he could add to discussions through using his reflections in ways that added to the quality of decision-making, rather than being seen as a negative dampener. However, in order to embed his story he needed to act on it. I asked him to find opportunities in his daily life where he could use his preferred style in support of delivering goals that mattered to him (no matter how small). He became adept at judging the moment when to insert himself into the noise of discussion, in order to help the team move forward, rather than waiting until the 'right' moment and annoying his boss. However, when the team faced a business crisis, the noise got louder, and he found himself reverting to his old habits. At first, he shrank into becoming a silent critical presence, but he now had sufficient insight into the power of old habits that, by holding himself to account for delivering good outcomes, he was able to hold onto his new habits.

The need to address sustainability is underpinned by research in neuroscience. Sixty years ago, Donald Hebb developed the theory that it is through persistent repetition that synaptic connections become more efficient. That theory is now commonly summarized as 'neurons that fire together wire together'. It is through repeated action that stronger and stronger neural circuits are built. This explains why clients have to have their story reinforced many times before it is wired strongly enough to sustain itself when the old story fires up again. It is important to help clients to understand that when the old habit reappears it is not a sign of failure but a signal that the new story requires added support, which can only come from sticking with it.

Reinforcers

When clients have worked through the process of creating a new narrative, I ask them to choose a symbol of the shift that will help sustain them once coaching comes to an end, and in those moments when the old story reappears. Something they can keep close, which will keep them on track. Some choose a poem, such as William Ernest Henley's poem 'Invictus', with its inspirational line, 'I am the master of my fate, I am the captain of my soul', or a quote from a powerful figure such as Mandela or Churchill. Others choose an object that holds meaning for them and can sit on their desk. One client selected a picture of a mediaeval cathedral. Its purpose was to remind him that he was a master craftsman not an apprentice, and that he no longer had to act as though he was an apprentice when challenged.

Invite your client to identify something that is meaningful to them and which will help them cement their new story into their neural circuits. Encourage them to be creative, as clients can struggle to think laterally. The selected object, song, picture or quote is only important for its relevance and value to the client. It does not have to represent high art, literature or worthiness. If they continue to struggle, then offering a range of postcard images can help broaden thinking. If they choose one of your images, that's fine; but they may instead refine the sort of image that would speak to them and become motivated to go and find it.

Summary

This chapter has built on the idea of the coach as enabling the client to write and articulate their narrative by focusing on the coach's role in the creation of a new narrative. It has done this by:

- Positioning a changed narrative as evolving in a wave formation where the move towards change is met by a cross current pushing the client back into the old story.
- Acknowledging that the old story does not disappear entirely, but is instead weakened by the growing power of a reinforced new story.
- Positioning the coach as being there to work with the reality of the change process by recognizing how the key constructs involved in the change process are playing out in each session.
- Moving the coach from the audience of the story to the challenger of the story, through calling on the range of coaching approaches that they have confidence in.
- Ensuring that the issue of sustainability is addressed, through acknowledging that old habits reappear at times of stress, and supporting the client in finding means by which they can self-support when coaching finishes.

The remainder of this book offers you a range of choices as to how you can work with clients on building the resources from which a new narrative emerges.

5 Cognitive behavioural therapy and resilience

You are listening to a client's account of the difficulty they face. They are presenting their version of the truth with such certainty that you are struggling to find a way in to begin challenging them. You want to help them find a way of viewing themselves and their situation from a vantage point that will open up choices and release some energy for action. In situations like this, cognitive behavioural therapy offers a way of working.

What is cognitive behavioural therapy?

Cognitive behavioural therapy (CBT) grew out of the work of two people: psychiatrist Aaron Beck and psychologist Albert Ellis. They came to similar conclusions as to why their clients were trapped in thinking patterns that allowed them no escape. Ellis argued that how individuals interpret events is shaped by core belief systems about themselves and how the world operates. Ellis saw these beliefs as faulty 'musts': for example, that everyone must think I am perfect or else I am worthless; that everyone must act the way I want them to act or I cannot accept them; or that the universe must give me what I want and how I want it or my life is intolerable. These beliefs, left unchallenged, shape emotional reactions and how people behave. Therefore, it followed, that if clients could be helped to recognize those beliefs, they could apply their cognitive skills to assess their validity. This would then equip them to create more useful beliefs that would support the changes they wanted to achieve.

Their thinking is captured in the often-quoted line from the Greek philosopher Epictetus that it is not events, but our beliefs about them, that causes us suffering. It is the creation of beliefs, or assumptions about our self, others, and the world that drives our actions, rather than events having an inevitable consequence. This reasoning explains why each day we see people reacting very differently to what on paper looks like the same challenge. One person approaching a significant birthday will decide to celebrate their increasing years. Another will deny it is happening, refuse to mark the day, and be gloomy for months beforehand. Regardless of how the person reacts, the birthday will happen. There are no automatic consequences, but we can create consequences that do not serve us well. If a client can be helped to recognize the limitations of their cognitive model on their actions, and can be enabled to change those cognitions, then their behavioural choices will be increased. Although CBT was developed for clinical settings and is now widely used within the NHS to work with a range of mental health issues, its principles have been extended into non-clinical populations, where it is labelled cognitive behavioural coaching.

The relevance of CBT to resilience

I am often struck by the certainties that clients bring to their accounts. They may tell a story of martyrdom, where whatever has happened is not their fault, and therefore there is nothing they could or should do about it. Or, they ask 'why me?' with the implicit message, 'I don't deserve this, it's unfair', which implies that until the world becomes fairer there is nothing they can do. Or, they present themselves as a failure, and with that knowledge there is no point in taking action since it will only lead to further failure. What each position is signalling is a lack of confidence in their own resources to make any difference to their future. Contrast this with the experience of Brian Keenan, an Irish teacher held captive in Beirut for four and a half years. He did not know when his imprisonment would end, or whether he would be killed. He did not know if he was being searched for, since government policy was not to negotiate with kidnappers. On the surface his position was powerless, and yet he held a position throughout his capture that he would be treated as an individual with rights. He made demands of his captors over how he was treated, and they came to accept them. That stance protected him, and kept him committed to getting through and getting out. Although Brian's circumstances were exceptional, the choices he faced are the same one's our clients face when life throws them a curve ball. Are they crushed by it, or do they acknowledge what has happened and then look to find ways of moving forward? Brian had to find a way of developing his own sustaining beliefs. As coaches we can use techniques from CBT to help individuals access theirs.

What happens to thinking when resilience goes?

Resilience is linked to flexibility in thinking. What marks our thinking when we lose access to resilience is that thoughts become distorted and with that distortion choices become restricted. Aaron Beck identified seven thinking traps he saw in his patients. I have seen them all when coaching clients. As you read them consider which you see in yours.

Jumping ahead

One piece of data is extrapolated into having a much wider meaning. An unreturned phone call means a person's boss has no time for them. A message that their boss wants to see them on Friday afternoon means they have done something wrong which will ruin their weekend. A colleague fails to acknowledge them as they enter the meeting and they assume they have offended them. The speed at which the conclusion is drawn does not allow for any space for considering alternatives: their boss prefers to discuss things face to face, there may be good news waiting for them, or the colleague may just be an introverted thinker preparing their thoughts before a meeting.

Partial vision

The individual scans situations with an eye to only noticing what is wrong. They will report back that a presentation was a disaster because the technology failed and they were not able to use the PowerPoint slides they had prepared. They will view their credibility as having been reduced. What they will not have noticed is that their audience was relieved not to have received a PowerPoint presentation. They did not recognize that by abandoning visual props they were able to make the session more interactive. They remember the one difficult question, but not those nodding in agreement with them. What could have been confidence-building because they are able to 'wing it' has become confidence-sapping because their focus was on fixed beliefs about what an effective presentation to senior leaders should look like.

Using the wrong lens

The individual is like a cameraman who constantly uses the wrong lens. Their account of events adopts a close-up lens on what is not okay so that it is magnified, and a long-distance lens on what is okay so that it is difficult to see or is blurred. They will report back on an experiment they have agreed to undertake giving great detail on how they did it wrong, how they did not follow the plan discussed, and then casually state that they got the outcome they wanted. When questioned on the successful outcome, they will dismiss their own role, attributing it to the largesse or good humour of the other person, or dismiss the outcome as 'no big deal'.

It's personal

This view positions the client as the cause of the problem, even if they have no direct influence over it. Their explanation of any situation is in terms of themselves, ignoring wider systemic factors over which they may have little control, or the idea of shared responsibility. The reason the client contract was lost is solely down to them. The reason they didn't get the promotion is exclusively because of what they did or did not do, and is unconnected to restructuring of the business. The reason they do not have a good relationship with a colleague is because of something they said at their first encounter. Personalizing could be seen as supporting resilience because holding an internal locus of control means that if you are the cause of the problem, you can also be the author of the solution. It does not work this way when resilience is lacking. When self-efficacy is absent, viewing issues as personal heightens the sense of helplessness.

Blaming

If internalization leads to helplessness, then externalization can do the same. Viewing everything as other people's fault also causes problems. Explaining outcomes in terms of recession, the government, the failures of a boss, their team or a client provides a false sense of comfort. It provides an excuse for doing nothing and staying stuck.

Generalizing

Generalizing occurs when people link problems to the character of those they deal with rather than focusing on their behaviour. If a colleague fails to deliver a good quality report, they describe that individual as hopeless, rather than someone who needs help to write better reports. As a hopeless colleague will inevitably always fail to deliver, the work will revert back to them. Since the issue they were bringing to the coaching was stress caused by their inability to handle their workload, they have just shot themselves in the foot. Alternately, they will generalize about their own capability, concluding that because they could not get support for additional resources, they are a failure as a leader.

Prophecy

The power of foresight is one that is valued – remember the Queen's question to embarrassed Bank of England officials: 'Why did no one see the recession coming?' Prophecy would seem to be a useful gift, but when we use it on ourselves we create self-fulfilling prophecies that can limit our options. A mid-career woman sees the most senior woman in the company leave, and predicts that no woman will ever make it to the top because men do not want women in positions of power. She then adjusts her career expectations downwards. A male colleague sees a woman appointed to the grade he aspires to as a result of external recruitment, and concludes that the CEO wants women in order to look good to the outside world, and therefore his career will plateau. The reality may be very different. The senior woman may only have ever wanted a two-year experience in that sector, and a change of strategy may explain the external recruitment. The facts do not matter. It is the power given to unexamined prophecies that does.

Working with distorted thinking

The thinking habits described above are ones we all engage in. Most of the time, we are able to counter them. I own up to having partial vision, but most of the time I have an innate optimism that quickly looks for the 'what else?' to counter the negative. You may start from experiencing setback as personal, but then bring in your analytical self and recognize the wider factors that explain the outcome. There are self-correcting mechanisms that when resourced, we are able to access in order to keep a balanced perspective. When resilience goes, clients become stuck with particular thinking patterns that are fuelled by deep-seated beliefs.

You may have recognized all of the above thinking habits in your clients, but holding on to seven patterns – and spotting them in a coaching session – is a challenge. However, in their writings on resilience, stress experts John Humphrey and Adrienne Green have condensed the seven patterns into what they call the 3 Ps: permanent, pervasive, and personal.

Permanent

Is the client talking in ways that suggest the situation will never change? Is their speech peppered by 'never' and 'always': 'I will never have enough money'; 'I will never get a job in an organization as good as my last'; 'I will always get overlooked because I don't network'. Alternatively, do they look to the past for evidence to bolster their view of the future? Because they had difficulties asserting themselves with a previous boss, do they assume they will never be able to assert themselves with people in authority? Permanent thinking leads to helplessness.

Pervasive

Is the client showing an inability to differentiate between experiences, so that if they made a bad choice in joining one organization, they see themselves as being a poor judge in any future option? Are they signalling in their account that they don't trust themselves, or that the world is a place they cannot trust, because they feel as though they have no control.

Personal

Is the client claiming that whenever something bad happens, it is their fault? Are they giving themselves powers of control over events that they cannot have? If a social event does not work out, is it their fault alone that their friends did not have a good time? If they are working long hours because of relentless deadlines, is it their fault because they don't work smart, rather than having any connection to inadequate resources or poor prioritization?

In moving clients away from the power of their existing thinking patterns, as a coach you want to enable the replacement of permanence with flexibility, and to shift thinking from pervasiveness to recognizing that situations are specific. You want your clients to recognize that bad things do happen, but that there are limits to what an individual is directly accountable for. Cognitive behavioural therapy has proved popular because it offers an approach that allows the client to start hearing their beliefs and to see the impact on their choices.

Working within a CBT framework

A key model in CBT work relates to the separation out of the situation, the consequence the person has created, and the belief that sits between the two. This is most simply expressed as the ABC model:

Adversity   What is the triggering event that has caused the response in the client?

Beliefs   What are the beliefs that the person attaches to themselves in relation to the event?

Consequence   What is the consequence that the individual has created as a result of their belief?

For the client, the process does not consciously follow from A to B to C. In the moment, the person jumps from A to C, with often very little awareness of the intervening B. To them their response is the natural consequence of what has happened to them. It can be a pattern that they have played out so often that their neural circuits are superconductors of this response. Your role is to make them aware of the process they have created, so that they can slow down their thinking and engage their cognitive skills.

Case study: Working with ABC

Katharine was a client who was referred by her boss because he was concerned at how distressed she became every time she submitted a piece of work to the head of the organization. She was often writing documents that would influence policy, and she would regularly work an eighty-hour week in order to produce a perfect piece of work. When the work was submitted and questions were raised, she would become emotional at the challenge and state that she was a failure.

Upon examining her ABC, we found that her parents, who were Holocaust survivors, had shaped her beliefs about perfection. Their response to survival had been to create a life that involved minimal risk through always doing the right thing. They had instilled in Katherine the belief that if you never make a mistake, you will be safe. The consequence was that she saw any questioning of her work as signalling that she was not safe, and therefore real feelings of fear were elicited.

When she slowed down and worked through the framework she was able to see that a belief system that made sense for her parents, limited her as an adult. She was able to create an alternative belief system that helped her create different consequences. Her new belief was that her work was good and any questioning of it did not make it valueless. With that belief she was able to recognize the point at which she should stop working on a document, thus reducing the number of hours she worked. She was also able to keep listening when in dialogue with the CEO, so that she was responsive rather than tearful.

In Katherine's work on her ABC, examining beliefs did not lead to the creation of a polar opposite. She did not move from 'my work has to be perfect' to 'my work can be mediocre', or from 'no-one should question me' to 'anyone can challenge me'. Neither of these responses would have convinced her, or created consequences she could live with. Instead, she explored alternatives that felt realistic and authentic to her. Accepting that her work had quality but that others had the right to question it opened up choices in both how she approached her work and how she managed others' responses to it. It also helped her to recognize that beliefs instilled in us by our parents should be respected for reflecting the truth of their experience, but may not be appropriate for ours.

Introducing the CBT framework

While the idea that one chooses what one thinks may be a comfortable one for a coach, a client stuck in the middle of difficulty may struggle to see they have any choice. In introducing the CBT framework, I sometimes ask the client what they would do if they looked out of the office door and saw a tiger walking down the corridor. Their response is usually that they would immediately close the door, hide in a corner, and look for a phone. To them that is the only plausible response. I then ask them what they think David Attenborough would do? Most believe his response would be very different: fear would be replaced with curiosity. Contrasting reactions allows them to recognize that without realizing it, they hold beliefs about tigers: that they are dangerous and life-threatening. Those beliefs shape their instinctive response to lock the door. In contrast, a wildlife expert would bring his fascination with large cats, and a belief that that he could, with care, manage himself in close proximity to it.

An alternative option is to introduce the idea of separate selves that co-exist within us: the 'I' that does things and the 'me' that comments on the 'I'. The idea of a self that takes action and a judging self that offers a running commentary is one that clients will recognize. They know the voice that says, 'you've messed up', 'why are you so stupid?', 'they are better than you'. However, they often see this judging self as a separate person over whom they have no control, and who holds the truth, rather than being their own creation. Chapter 7 looks at working with these selves through the lens of mindfulness. From a CBT perspective, positioning that judging self as a voice that holds beliefs about how that person should be, and recognizing it is the product of their own creation allows it to be challenged within the ABC framework.

Exercise 5.1: ABC exercise

Invite the client to talk through a current adversity using the template in Table 5.1. Invite them to jot down their responses on the template once they have talked them through with you. Note that in the first iteration, you invite the client to go A-C-B, in order to help them recognize that the consequence was a direct, if unacknowledged, response to their beliefs.

Table 5.1 Example of ABC

Adversity: the what, where, and when	Consequence	Belief
I received negative feedback from the Chair about my behaviour in a meeting with the Board.	Argued against the feedback. Decided that the only thing I could do was look for another job, so I registered with a headhunter.	You must never admit to mistakes. My career is over. I won't be forgiven. **Permanent and Pervasive thinking**

Assuming that the individual's preferred outcome would be to find a way of remaining with the organization, and mending fences, the exercise is then repeated. This time the client is invited to identify alternative realistic and authentic beliefs that could be applied to the adversity (see Table 5.2).

Key to the effectiveness of the ABC model is the willingness of the individual to act on the consequences that result from a shift in beliefs. Only when they experience a different outcome by taking different beliefs back to the situation will they integrate the new belief. As a coach, you need to be confident that the client is capable of acting on their new consequences. Their model needs to be tested, so that they have the opportunity not only to rehearse action, but also to recognize if the belief is realistic and authentic.

Table 5.2 Challenging the ABC

Adversity: the what, where, and when	Belief: Authentic and Realistic	Consequence
I received negative feedback from the Chair about my behaviour in a meeting with the Board.	If they give me feedback they are offering me the chance to put it right. If I can put it right, this episode will be forgotten over time. I may have got it wrong but I am capable of learning. **Flexible thinking**	Apologizes to the Chair for getting it wrong this time. Asks another Board member for input on where he saw him getting it wrong. Develops a strategy for not losing control when the argument becomes heated in the boardroom. Seeks feedback after his next boardroom appearance.

Testing may reveal that they have not bottomed out the real alternative and motivating belief, or that the scale of action is beyond their capability at this point. This allows for beliefs to be re-visited until the client is convinced by their own thoughts.

Alternatively, it may reveal that the strength of the judging voice is so strong that it cannot be made silent through cognition alone. When this happens, it can be useful to look at other ways of quietening the voice. Chapter 6, which looks at Acceptance and Commitment Therapy, offers an alternative approach.

Is CBT more than ABC?

In contrast to the attention given in the CBT literature to helping people adjust distorted thinking, little attention has been given to its potential to help people recognize strengths that could be of value to them in working through tough times. However, since we are resilient most of the time, it follows that we have developed strengths that we use constantly to help us deal with the 'ups and downs' of our daily lives. The sense of humour that allows us to quickly recover from a mishap, the creativity that enables us to reconfigure our time when plans are thrown up in the air by a sudden emergency, or the flexibility that enables us to sort out how we are going to get to a destination when the train breaks down.

When a client is in the middle of a challenging situation, they lose contact with those strengths. A coach can help them see what is available that is of value in building their resilience toolkit. We can do this by working through four steps that focus on accessing strengths. These steps were developed by clinical psychologist Christine Padesky, but are equally applicable within coaching.

Step 1

Look for strengths that are available to the client in situations unrelated to their present challenge. Encourage the client to look for them in hobbies, in their daily habits or in areas linked to their values. This will mean slowing the client down to really unpick what they do in as much detail as possible.

Step 2

Construct with them a personal resilience model based on the strengths identified in Step 1. What skills and strengths have they already noted, but which are not being attached to the current situation. Ensure the model uses their words and not your interpretation of their words.

Step 3

Invite the client to consider how they could better maintain resilience in the face of their current difficulty by using the strengths they have identified in Step 2. The focus here is not on how they can overcome the difficulty using the strengths they have identified, but how they can use them to *persist* in the face of the difficulty. The solution may not yet be visible, so the need is to persist until the solution emerges.

Step 4

Practise resilience by agreeing a behavioural experiment using the personal resilience model. Ask the client to predict how they think their resilience will play out in the situation. For example, how long do they imagine they will be able to hold their space in a difficult conversation? How do they think their resilience will look and feel in the moment? What will they be thinking after the conversation? The aim is not to focus on the outcome of the encounter, but to focus on their resilience within the encounter.

Case study: Coaching the 4 Steps Model

Corinne's exit from a senior role had been painful, and it was made even more so by it being reported in the press. After a career that had been marked by her commitment and success, this was the first time she had 'failed' and she was devastated. Her attempts to find a new role were proving difficult, and she carried with her into each interview the belief that no one would want damaged goods. It was difficult to get her to move beyond her story of failure, so I turned to the four steps to see if they would help her unstick herself.

In Step 1, I unearthed that she had a passion for helping families with disabled children. Despite her demanding lifestyle, she had always found ways of giving respite care. The strengths that she drew on were her religious faith, her desire to focus on what was possible for each child, her belief in the interconnectedness of humanity, and her willingness to stretch out and give a helping hand without being asked to. She also acknowledged the strength she had shown in never giving up on voluntary work even when the demands of her day job were high.

In Step 2, she built her personal resilience model, which encompassed her persistence, her offering of support, her seeing people as equal, her optimism, her faith, and her belief that there was more to life than work.

In Step 3, she looked at her own situation and saw that by applying her strengths, she could retain a sense of optimism about future possibilities even though she did not know what the outcome would be. She could equally stretch out her hand and ask for help just as she so easily offered her help to others. She was able to see that although work was important, it was not the only way in which she valued herself, and that maybe, in the future, she will want a different balance in her life.

With trust in her own model, she was then able to take Step 4 and think of ways in which she could experiment. She contacted former colleagues and told them about her situation, and found them anxious to help her by putting her in touch with contacts. When she met with these contacts, she discovered that they did not look at her past story of failure, but were more engaged by wanting to help her succeed. She was able to devote time to her voluntary work rather than spending her days worrying about not having a job. Her big behavioural experiment was to go out to lunch with a colleague from her former employer. Her challenge was to stay resilient while not pretending her life was sorted. Although she would have liked to have been able to report having a new job and reflect that leaving the company was the best thing that ever happened to her, that was not the reality. Being able to report back that she was able to be herself, and that she connected with her colleague on an equal basis knowing that bad things happen to good people, helped her to stay resilient until a new role emerged.

The four steps did not produce a solution, but they helped her regain resilience so that she could better deal with the uncertainty of her unresolved future.

When CBT isn't the right choice

Cognitive behavioural therapy divides clinicians. Some see it as an effective short-term intervention, others as a cost-led, mechanistic, poorly executed intervention that does not lead to sustainable outcomes. Although coaches are not working with clients who have severe depression or bipolar disorders, it is still important to assess its validity for use with a particular client. When a client presents with an issue that has at its heart a resilience gap, you have to decide if CBT is the best way of helping them to address that gap.

A key argument of this book is that resilience is about a temporary loss of functioning in relation to a specific event. You therefore need to have evidence that the person is functioning effectively in other areas of their life. If they are not, then you have a responsibility to refer them on for specialist help. For example, in working with one client it emerged that the negative beliefs he brought to his ability to get over a knock-back at work extended to every aspect of his life. Working with beliefs about his work performance was of no value until he had been helped by a clinician to address the depression that was a black cloud over his life.

If you are convinced that the client is bringing a single issue to their work with you, then CBT can be a useful means of enabling the development of new models and accessing hidden strengths. But even if a client passes the single issue test, there will be those for whom CBT does not connect. Implicit to the idea of reframing beliefs is an acknowledgement by the client that they have a locus of control that allows them to make choices. When a client will not accept their responsibility, the framework will not work. I worked with a woman who had built her career by following a boss from job to job. When he was asked to resign by a new CEO, she felt bereft. She had externalized responsibility for her life onto him, and when he was no longer there she became angry with her employer, and then with me for asking her to take responsibility and to challenge her thinking. Her anger showed itself in an eagerness to agree actions followed within hours by emails informing me that I had completely misunderstood her, and the actions agreed were impossible. When I confronted her about the pattern of our sessions, she decided our work together should end.

The timing of the introduction of CBT is also central. A client who has just been told that their performance is inadequate or that they are to be made redundant is unlikely to respond well to an invitation to bolster their resilience by looking at distorted thinking. They need to be allowed to be sad or angry, to rage against the world and to cry tears of fear, while feeling supported and listened to. The time to introduce CBT is the moment they recognize that their thoughts about themselves and their future are holding them back.

As much as CBT can be the wrong choice for a client because of timing or an unwillingness to see themselves as an agent in their own life, it can be the wrong choice for a coach. The focus on cognition can appeal to coaches who are unsettled by strong emotions in their clients. Just focusing on cognitions can be used to limit the emotions that the client brings into the coaching space. In contrast, it is often through enabling the client to explore their emotional responses that they are able to re-engage more constructively with their cognitions. When a coach operates CBT as a framework to manage the client's emotional disclosure, its purpose is to protect the coach from losing their own resilience in the face of what they find challenging. A question you should ask yourself is in whose interest is CBT being used?

Summary

In looking at the place of cognitive behavioural approaches to working with resilience issues, this chapter has examined:

- The core principles underpinning CBT.
- The distorted thought patterns that influence loss of resilience.
- The ABC framework and how it can be used in coaching to open up choices.
- Using a CBT approach to finding strengths that will support persistence in the face of difficulty.
- When CBT is the right choice and when it is not.

6 Acceptance and commitment therapy and resilience

The film 'The Full Monty' told the story of six Sheffield steelworkers who when the steelworks closed decided that they would earn money as a group of male strippers. In the process they found friendship, focus, and renewed self-esteem. Within the film was a sub-plot. Gerald, the only one to have held an office job could not accept the loss of his job. Each day he dressed for work, left the house and returned at the end of the day, pretending to himself and his wife that he was still employed. He was experiencing what I often see in clients: an inability to face a difficult reality. By acting as though he was still employed, he hoped to protect himself from feelings of shame. Our clients may not need to pretend to be employed but they can be equally adept at avoiding difficult truths. They can deny the evidence of 360-degree feedback, deny that the organization is looking at younger talent, or deny that if they don't change their behaviour and up their game they are at risk. Clients are often caught in the reality gap between what is and what they would like. A common reaction is to deny that gap because of not wanting to experience the pain that goes with recognition. Acceptance and commitment therapy (ACT) has a place in working with such clients, because it takes as its starting point the fact that life has inescapable difficulties that bring us suffering. The need is not to deny difficulties or reframe them, to look for silver linings or to chant positive affirmations, but to accept they exist. The client does not need to change anything – they simply need to learn to live with their discomfort, and to experience what follows from that acceptance.

The relevance of acceptance and commitment therapy for working with resilience issues

Andrea Redmond and Patricia Crisafulli interviewed business leaders who had not only been fired, but their setbacks had been front-page news in the business press. What was notable in their accounts of how they recovered and moved on was the importance of facing reality. While the immediate reaction was often to withdraw or to blame others, key to their accounts was the point at which they faced reality: the reality not only that they had visibly failed but that they had had a part to play in that process. While the unconditional love and support of their friends was important, the point at which they started to open up to what they could be beyond failure was when they accepted failure and the pain of that failure. They came to that recognition alone, but as coaches we can help our clients to engage with reality. Acceptance and commitment therapy provides tools to enable clients to look at their issue and the pain they associate with it. Where a client cannot engage with the idea of changing their thoughts, or where attempts to do so end in failure, ACT offers another option, to learn how to be with those thoughts and feelings.

What is acceptance and commitment therapy?

Acceptance and commitment therapy resides in the tradition of cognitive therapy, but it takes it in a new direction. Its roots lie in the work of Steven Hayes, an academic psychologist who developed relational frame theory (RFT). Although RFT is a theory of enormous linguistic complexity, at its heart is the belief that our language creates human suffering: the language we use in the public domain through writing, speech, and gestures, but particularly our private language – in our thinking, planning, worrying, daydreaming, analysing, and fantasizing. For Hayes, the mind is a complex system of processes such as comparing, evaluating, judging, and visualizing, all of which rely on human language. While that language can be helpful to us, it also has a dark side in that it can deceive us, cause us to relive painful events, scare us with fears of the future, and lead us to judge ourselves.

Whereas CBT looks to deal with that language by challenging it, ACT sees the need as being to recognize that living a rich and meaningful life involves accepting the pain that goes with it. It is here that ACT makes a link with mindfulness (explored more fully in the next chapter), and the Buddhist precept of the inevitability of suffering, as part of the human experience. Acceptance challenges the idea that through being good, setting goals, working hard, being successful or living healthily we can avoid experiencing emotional pain. It is a direct challenge to self-help books that position themselves as helping us to live a life where pain can be eradicated by taking control of our career, our weight, and our relationships. Instead, it argues that it is our avoidance of accepting pain that leads us into self-defeating behaviours. Life has to be lived experiencing the full gamut of human emotions. Rather than seeking to create life as a calm sea on a sunny day, accept that like the sea the conditions of our lives are constantly changing.

Unlike other cognitive approaches, ACT does not look to reduce symptoms, because it argues that it is the focus on symptoms that sets up the struggle within an individual to rid themselves of those symptoms. Our desire not to feel awkward, embarrassed, shameful or guilty leads us to push those feelings away, but perversely strengthens our connection to them. Instead, symptoms reduce as a by-product of moving into a mindful relationship with the difficulty. By being able to separate from thoughts and feelings and simply observe them and recognize their transience, the client can be helped to connect with values to guide their actions. Connecting with values provides the purpose that allows individuals to shift, without needing to change thoughts.

A client who labelled himself as socially awkward, even as he wanted to connect with people, pushed away feelings of social awkwardness by avoiding social situations that called for 'small talk'. He was inventive in finding ways of turning down social invitations, but that skill only increased his anxiety every time an invitation arrived in his inbox. Instead of avoiding social events, which only increased his sense of isolation and lack of social skills, his need was to change his relationship with the thoughts and feelings that went with social situations. By helping him to see his social awkwardness as not present all of the time, and to accept it as a harmless but at times uncomfortable experience, I was able to invite him to consider his willingness to face the discomfort of a social event in the service of his desire for closer relationships with people. He was not asked to reframe the social event as a fun evening or to see himself as socially adept. Instead, he was asked to be willing to face the thoughts and feelings of social awkwardness in the support of achieving something he wanted. That mindset enabled him to take the risk of going to an end-of-project celebration and to stay for one hour. In that hour he discovered that not every minute was painful, and he established a starting point for building social contact.

What happens when we cannot be present

Acceptance and commitment therapy positions itself as mindfulness-based practice based on a cognitive theory. The place of mindfulness in ACT can be understood through looking at six core responses, which it argues keep clients trapped in psychological inflexibility. Those inflexibilities all develop from an inability to be with the present.

Fusion

Fusion occurs when clients become entangled in particular thoughts that then dominate how they see the world and how they behave within it. They become fused with thoughts and feelings about themselves from the past: feelings such as rejection, disappointment or failure. Rather than having a range of thoughts available to them, the client becomes attached to particular thoughts they play over and over again. I hear fusion in clients who will talk of a past failure as defining who they are many years later, or how they will never achieve a goal because of a future they have already created.

Experiential avoidance

Experiential avoidance is the attempt to escape unwanted thoughts, feelings or memories. So as not to feel anxious, sad, angry, ashamed or lonely, the client avoids putting themselves into situations where they could experience them. The job-seeker stops applying for jobs because of not wanting to experience feelings of rejection. Someone wanting a partner stops going out because of not wanting to experience disappointment. A coach fails to send out evaluation forms because knowing the coaching relationship did not go well, they don't want to face the feelings of failure. The more time spent avoiding or trying to get rid of private thoughts, the greater the suffering in the long term. It is like skiing down a slope that frightens you: follow your instinct and lean backwards, avoiding looking down the hill, and you will fall, increasing your fear. Lean into the slope and look ahead, and while the feelings of fear will stay with you, you are likely to arrive at the bottom unscathed, knowing you can ski well with fear.

Dominance of the past or future

In losing connection with the present, clients seek out particular memories from their past. They create a past that focuses on negatives, or which only picks up on data that support the logic of the present difficulty. Alternatively, they can create a future based on past failing and inadequacy, and only see what can go wrong. Clients will trawl back into their history to recall an event that they see as mirroring their present, and then extend it into a psychic interpretation of what this means for their future.

Lack of certainty over values

When individuals are caught up in a difficult present, resistance to which is using up all their mental energies, they can lose sight of their values. In doing so, they no longer have a compass to direct their energies. Someone who holds a value about the importance of helping others can be so caught up in themselves that they fail to notice when others need help. Someone who has lost confidence because of a poor relationship with their boss and is obsessing over what they should have done, can be blind to the fact that their work no longer matches who they are.

Unworkable actions

Unworkable actions are those things that take us away from the present and the thoughts and feelings of the moment. They offer short-term relief while in reality increasing our difficulties. It can lead us to drinking more than usual, shopping online beyond our resources, eating comfort foods as a daily reward, gambling in the hope of experiencing the excitement of a win, sleeping away weekends, taking drugs to numb feelings, or spending night after night closing down our mind by watching mindless TV. There are days when not answering the phone to avoid a difficult conversation, or having the extra glass of wine to relax makes sense, but when the action becomes habitual and is stopping us from dealing with difficulty, then it has become unworkable.

Attachment to a conceptualized self

The conceptualized self is a story which has been created about the self and which has become rigid. This is more than a story attached to a particular event; it is a story about who the person is in the world. When people are experiencing difficulty, the conceptualized self they may access is one that reports back to them that they are worthless, stupid, unlovable, boring, fat, damaged goods or a loser. The story is one-dimensional but explains to the client why things are as they are. Conversely, a person whose conceptualized self is of being strong, smart or autonomous can be equally ill-served when life throws them a curve ball, and they are knocked by discovering that their reactions do not square with who they thought they were.

What do you notice in your clients?

Before looking at how to help clients build psychological flexibility through ACT, reflect on the core pathologies in relation to your client work.

Consider a client who is struggling with a difficult reality at the moment (that client could even be you):

1. *Fusion.* What sort of unhelpful cognitions are they fused to? For example, do they hold rigid rules about how they have to be,

express strong judgements about themselves or hold unrealistic expectations of how others should be?

2. *Experiential avoidance.* What feelings or thoughts are your client avoiding? What do you notice they are shying away from? How are they doing avoidance?

3. *Dominance of the conceptualized past or future.* How much time do they spend dwelling on the past or fantasizing the future?

4. *Values.* Do you know what your client's values are? Do they talk of values in relation to how they live their lives? Does the idea of having values to guide them leave them confused? Have they abandoned their values, or put them on hold?

5. *Unworkable action.* What self-defeating actions is your client taking? Are they persisting with actions that have no chance of success in order to avoid facing reality? Are they numbing their feelings about the present by legal or non-legal means?

6. *Attachment to the conceptualized self.* What does the client bring to sessions that hinders their moving on? Do they see themselves as 'past it', superior, ruined, stupid, successful or strong? Are they fused to a body image of themselves, such as being a fat middle-aged man/woman that defines them in the world, or are they attached to a particular role that they must have in order to be validated?

The logic of ACT is that as coaches we need to help our clients be with the present moment, to accept difficult feelings and thoughts, and to separate from the stories they hold about themselves and their situation. Our role is to connect them with values that will enable them to choose actions that are helpful, and to hold back from wanting our clients to change in order not to be in pain. How do we do that?

Contacting the present moment

Mindfulness has at its core a connection with the present moment, and the following chapter offers ways of facilitating this, using exercises drawn from meditative practices. However, ACT sees the client and coach as in a creative partnership, where the coach can create exercises that are based on mindfulness principles and that match with the style and needs of the individual client. It does not ask that the client commit to a set amount of time to meditate each day. It opens up space for short exercises that can be taught within sessions. Psychotherapist and writer Russ Harris, a key writer on ACT, is inventive in devising ways in which concepts can be made workable for clients. His books offer examples to help a client be with the present. One exercise I have developed is designed to help clients come back to the present moment when they find themselves becoming overwhelmed by thoughts that are preventing them dealing with what is at hand.

Exercise 6.1: Grounding exercise

Invite your client to sit in a chair with their eyes open. Ask them to push their feet hard into the ground so that they feel the pressure of the ground on their feet. Ask them to sit upright with their spine against the chair rather than relaxing into it.

As they feel their feet pushed hard into the ground, invite them to take slow deep breaths. As they breathe, ask them to look around and note five things they can see. Then ask them to listen carefully and note five things they can hear. Then ask them to notice where they are right now and what they are doing.

This simple exercise is designed to get the client back into the present moment so that they can engage with the moment. If the person is not comfortable sitting, then they can do the exercise standing up, pushing their palms together hard as their grounding focus.

Grounding is a useful practice at the beginning of a session to get the client into being with the work of coaching, rather than whatever they have just left behind. Its simplicity means that a client can do it alone when they are feeling themselves becoming overwhelmed by thoughts.

Some years ago I was struggling. I had a well-established relationship with a large corporation and as a result the global HQ had asked me to design a programme for their senior managers. I carried out a diagnosis of need and then went back to present my findings. The presentation went badly, so badly that one person walked out of the room. I flew home dejected and spent days going over and over the event, punishing myself for my stupidity, but telling no one because of shame and a wish to deny the reality to myself. Eventually, I noticed that my body was in a constant state of tension and that when working on other client work my mind was constantly being flooded with my feelings of failure. As I sat at my desk, I grounded myself. I pushed my feet hard into the floor, took some deep breaths, tuned into the noises and sights around me, and as I did so I felt myself expand. With that space I felt able to recognize the job in hand. It enabled me to pick up the phone to my client, to acknowledge that I had misread the audience and to ask for feedback. When I put the phone down, the tension had gone. Regardless of whether they ever asked me to work with them again, I found that when I faced the wave it did not engulf me.

Defusion

When fused to an idea, it is impossible to see beyond it, and therefore impossible to acknowledge that there are any other thoughts available to us. Defusion is about helping the client step away from the thought and then neutralizing its impact. This process can be done in three steps: noticing, naming the story, and neutralizing.

Noticing

Acceptance and commitment therapy allows us to actively notice thoughts as we go about our daily life. I notice as I write this book that I catch myself having the 'it won't help coaches' thought, or 'the editor won't like this' thought, and in the conscious noticing of it, I am able to stand back and ask myself how will not seeing the book as useful or worrying about the editor's response help me write well? The starting point for defusing a client's thought is increasing their conscious awareness of it. You can do this within a session, and then ask your client to practise it several times a day.

Invite them to stop whatever they are doing and simply let their mind do what it wants to do. Within a session, allow a couple of minute's silence and then ask them to name the thoughts they were having. Rather than asking them to tell you what they were thinking about, ask them to categorize the thoughts. For example, feeling silly about sitting in silence is an embarrassment thought; replaying the argument last night is a reliving thought. Ask them to categorize the thoughts they had in those two minutes and to then assess how useful they are to them right now. This in itself can help clients recognize how often thoughts are not helpful to our purpose. Teaching this technique is useful when the client notices that their thoughts are undermining them, but feel stuck with those thoughts. It helps them to see thoughts as objects that are defused by noticing them rather than being mind-bombs.

Naming the story

Naming the story links the client with the issue they are bringing to you. Invite them to notice the thoughts they most often hold about the issue. Then invite them to imagine that they are writing a story about the issue and want to signal to their readers the story they are about to read. What would the story be called? The title should be entitled 'The … Story', with the title capturing truthfully the story they carry within them. You may need to offer examples to give them confidence that you really want them to be honest, for example 'The Victim Story', 'The Loser Story', 'The Sidelined Story', 'The Not Good Enough Story'. Whatever title they choose, it should help them to notice when they are having the thought captured in the title. The aim is not to change the story title, but to notice when the 'Not Good Enough Story' starts up again, and to be curious as to what happens to the story when they notice it. For example, does the noticing of it allow for it to be challenged with an alternative version? The word curious is a useful one when introducing an experiment to a client because it has its origin in the Latin word *cura*, meaning care. Inviting your client to be curious is to invite them to enter the experiment with a mindset that will help them take care of themselves.

Neutralizing

Neutralizing is about taking away the power of the thought. There are many creative ways in which you can do this within ACT: asking the client to type out the thought in different font sizes and colours, drawing a cartoon figure saying the thought, saying it out loud in a silly voice, singing the thought to a well-known song or even emblazoning it on a T-shirt. Coaches can be creative in devising ways of putting the thought into a new context so that it loses its power. A client who was convinced he was too old to be offered a new role, and was highly introverted in his behaviour, neutralized his thought when I asked him to sing repeatedly 'I am too old to matter' silently inside his head to the tune of 'Happy Birthday to You'. He would never have sung it out loud. After a minute's silence, he looked at me and said: 'That is ridiculous, I am not too old, it's just an excuse.' This recognition did not stop him having the thought, but when he did he remembered his silent singing and the thought became ridiculous again.

Case study: Separating from the thought

Robert was a specialist who valued certainty. He related the story of a former boss who had announced on his arrival that he did not want specialists and expected people to move on into other areas of the business. To make the point, he introduced a tight performance management system. Robert left the organization rather than be examined, but several years later he discovered the 'ogre boss' was about to join his current employer. He came to me in a state of anxiety, fearing his past would catch up with him, and that his only option was to leave.

I introduced the idea that holding onto this story from the past was like someone holding on tightly to a precious object, and asked him to name all the thoughts and feelings that he held onto from that past experience. I then gave him a book and asked him to imagine that all the thoughts and feelings he held about himself in relation to that experience were in the book. I invited him to hold the book as close to his face as he could, blocking out his peripheral vision, and to experience the thoughts as ones he wanted to hold tightly onto. I then asked him to put the book on the floor some comfortable distance away from him, and to tell me anything he noticed or felt. With that distance he said he had different thoughts. He could see that he had stayed too long in the role and had become complacent, and that the move out had woken up his ambitions. When I asked him to put the book on his lap and breathe deeply, he noticed that he was experiencing himself differently again. This time he noticed himself as the person he now was, with enhanced skills and experience. He had experienced the confidence he had available to him to deal with whatever happened, rather than running from it.

Acceptance and opening up

Acceptance is about being able to recognize that the things we do in order to protect ourselves from painful feelings and thoughts do not work. It is about being able to help the client see that what they see as 'coping' strategies – allowing them to cling on – are not strategies for resolving the difficult. Clients will often offer, with a wry smile, a list of the things they are doing in order to 'get by', from buying expensive clothes as a reward for an unfulfilling life to relentless exercise in an attempt to exhaust themselves so they cannot think. Rather than colluding with their coping behaviours, the coach can ask them: what they are currently doing to keep going that could make their life worse in the long term; what they are doing that is keeping them stuck where they are; what they are doing that impacts negatively on their health or relationships; what they are doing that makes worse the problem they are wanting to address. By answering such questions, the coach invites the client to recognize the inadequacy of coping, and to face the pain of the issue at its starting point for finding a way through it.

Case study: Opening up to stop

George was a highly successful workaholic leader. He could work for twenty-four hours at a time. He sent emails at 3 am and was at his desk at 6 am. He seemed to know the briefs of his direct reports and colleagues better than they did, and there was no work challenge he was not willing to take on. What drove George was not ambition, but fear. He was the eldest of a large family, where he had been held responsible for his siblings while his mother worked. He took the responsibility seriously, but one day he decided to go to an additional session after school, and told his siblings to start cooking dinner before he came home. As he rounded the street corner he saw the fire engines outside the house. The kitchen was alight, and in his mind he was responsible. He became fused to a story of the need for him to take full responsibility in any situation, and the risks of not doing so. He was also fused with a self-concept of himself as the rescuer. It was only when he recognized that his emotional and mental energy could not sustain this way of working that he was able to begin to address his fusions. Accepting the power of feelings of fear experienced as a child was a difficult admission, but through acknowledging them he could begin to put distance between himself and the story, and start to consider the person he now was.

Connecting with values

Values are about knowing what matters to us, and trusting they are the basis for our decision-making. Values are central to ACT because by clarifying one's values, people can live meaningful lives, even if they cannot remove the difficulty. Without values people have no safe harbour when the going gets tough. Helping clients reconnect to values is important because it gives them a basis for taking actions that they are committed to.

Careers books and online resources contain many values exercises that can be useful in helping clients put a name to those things that drive their commitment. Acceptance and commitment therapy takes this a stage further by focusing on the extent to which the individual is living in accordance with those values.

Exercise 6.2: Dartboard exercise

This exercise is adapted with permission from the work of ACT therapist Tobias Lundgren.

Invite your client to consider the values that are important to them through conversation or by administering a values questionnaire. It is important to signal that no value is right or wrong, better or worse. Values generally fall into three categories:

- *Caring:* about someone or something
- *Connecting:* to someone or something
- *Contributing:* to something

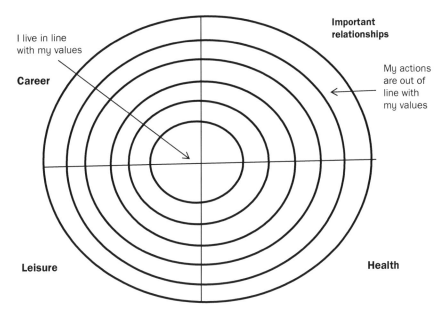

Figure 6.1   The values dartboard (Adapted with the permission of Tobias Lundgren)

> Once they have clarified their values, ask them to identify key areas of their life that are important to them. Figure 6.1 provides in illustration. It is important that they label the areas using their own language and criteria, and that there is no judgement attached to their categories. I once worked with a client whose cat was at the heart of her life, and so had a place on the dartboard. Whatever is important to the client is a focus for how far their living is in line with their values. Once they have placed their categories on the dartboard, invite them to consider how close to the bull's-eye they currently are in terms of how they apply their values to their living.

Clarifying values provides clients with an anchor: This is who I am regardless of what is whirling around me. Assessing the degree to which they are living in accordance with those values allows for the emergence of purpose, and what flows effortlessly from purpose is committed actions. Without setting goals, changed action follows from purpose. Without purpose, goals can remain un-acted dreams.

Case study: Connecting with values

Amanda had been encouraged from childhood to work hard and to succeed. Her family loved hearing that she had got a new promotion and that she could buy designer clothes. All appeared fine until Amanda received bruising feedback that signalled that she was not going to be appointed to her boss's position when he moved on. She felt betrayed, as he had used the carrot of his job to encourage her to deliver beyond her job description. She came to the sessions angry. She was refusing to help the new boss as revenge for being sidelined, and was enjoying watching him struggle. While her anger protected her from the pain of disappointment, it did not help her move on. It was an avoidance strategy. When we explored her values, it became clear that from her religious faith she had values related to connection and contribution that she took into her private life but she did not act on at work. When she recognized the gap, she began to look at her situation differently. She stopped demonizing her new boss, but also recognized that spending money on designer labels did not make her feel rewarded. It directed her away from plotting against an enemy to looking for more fulfilling work.

Committed action

Many coaching models focus on action as a measure of change; ACT does not do this. It sees action as a choice that can emerge from the process but it does not demand it. It starts from a focus on the power of acceptance, and an openness as to what can shift when someone accepts the situation they are in and applies their values to living with what is. When a client comes to us looking for a remedy for the pain of difficulty, we can engage with them in building a strategy for change, or we can ask them to accept the reality of what is, and explore what changes when that acceptance is linked to their values. This is not a resentful or grudging acceptance, but a positive, purposeful recognition of reality. It is seen in the terminally ill person who stops searching for a cure and focuses on how to make the best of the time they have. It is seen in the couple that accept their infertility and look at what life can now be without children. It is seen in the ambitious executive who accepts he may not achieve his potential because of supporting a teenage child with mental health issues.

When is ACT the right choice?

As clients come to us with issues they cannot resolve themselves, their immediate hope is that we can help them fix it. They may initially see the coach as a magician with tools to put it right. Even once they understand that the solution will be theirs, clients instinctively focus on finding a solution that gets them what they want. That is why it seems counter-intuitive to focus on acceptance. It is often only when the client has run through the gamut of other approaches that they are open to developing a different relationship with the issue. When they recognize that their brain refuses to see positives in negatives; when they recognize that knowing what you should do does not make it happen; when they accept that their coping strategies keep them afloat but don't equip them to swim – then they may be open to taking a different approach. Because ACT does not sit comfortably with models focused on goal-setting and planned actions towards outcomes, clients may require reassurance that it can work. Many studies have shown the effectiveness of ACT in working with conditions such as depression, workplace stress, anxiety, post-traumatic stress disorder, drug abuse, and obsessive compulsive disorder. While it is well established in clinical settings, its use in coaching has received much less attention.

For the coach, ACT requires sufficient experience of mindfulness that they are able to adapt it to meet the needs of particular clients. It asks that you have the confidence to be willing to sit with difficult thoughts and emotions in clients without wanting to defuse them for your own comfort. It demands that you do not collude with the idea that by taking action the client will remove the difficulty, or that before taking action the issue needs to have been removed. Instead, it tests the client's willingness to take action, accepting the pain that may be experienced, in the service of values about themselves and the way they want to live their life.

Summary

In looking at how ACT can add to your repertoire when working with resilience issues, the chapter has:

- Positioned ACT as a means of helping clients to confront unpleasant realities.
- Shifted the focus from how thoughts and emotions can be changed to how an individual can learn to accept the uncomfortable as the basis for moving forward.
- Described how coping strategies that provide short-term relief exacerbate the underlying issue.
- Shown how mindfulness combined with a focus on clarifying values provides the basis for the individual taking committed action regardless of circumstances.
- Provided exercises to support your clients' psychological flexibility.

7　Mindfulness and resilience

The previous chapter looked at acceptance and commitment therapy as a means of working with resilience issues. Key tenets of ACT are drawn from Buddhism, including the use of mindfulness practices as part of the process of acceptance. In this chapter, the focus is exclusively on the place of mindfulness in working with resilience issues, with the acknowledgement that it is a personal practice of many coaches, and is becoming an increasingly popular development input in high demand corporate settings. There are many advocates of mindfulness, and its popularity has inevitably led to a questioning of whether it is just another coaching 'fad'. In this chapter, it is examined from the perspective of its value when working with clients who have resilience gaps and who may have little if any awareness of mindfulness. The chapter also examines what is deliverable within a time-limited coaching contract.

What is mindfulness?

The most commonly cited definition of mindfulness is that provided by Jon Kabat-Zinn. A professor of medicine and practising Buddhist, Kabat-Zinn created the Stress Reduction Clinic at the University of Massachusetts Medical Center, and his influence on the application of mindfulness within and outside of health care settings has been profound. He defines mindfulness as 'paying attention in a particular way: on purpose, in the present moment, and non-judgmentally'. That one sentence is underpinned by a wealth of meaning. It focuses on the importance of giving focus to our thoughts and providing space for our thoughts. It places value on this moment, rather than giving our mind to the future or dwelling on the past. It puts the individual in the position of observer of self, rather than being caught in judging thoughts or feelings. It is also implicitly positioned as a means by which thoughts change, not through an act of will, but simply by the process of noticing that thoughts do not hold 'the truth'. They are simply thoughts, which change from moment to moment. Rick Hanson of the Wellspring Institute for Neuroscience describes it as a tool to 'train the mind, to change the brain to change the mind for the better'. It is a means by which people can make friends with their minds, rather than seeing themselves as governed and controlled by them.

Mindfulness is often associated with Buddhism, because of the idea of using meditation practices to develop a sense of being alive to the reality of the moment. That presence is the means of making peace with oneself and one's relationship with the world. In reality, mindfulness is a theme found in other religions, including Sufism and Taoism. Outside of religion, it is that capacity we see in children to be completely absorbed in the experience of jumping in and out of a muddy puddle, experiencing the physical sensations, thoughts, and emotions that are present for them, while their parents badger them to 'hurry up' because the parents' thoughts and attention are on to the next thing that needs doing. As adults, we are rarely present. Instead, we constantly wander back in our thoughts as though we can undo what has been done, and wander forward as though we can predict the future. When Matthew Killingsworth and Daniel Gilbert, two scientists with an interest in happiness, used an Iphone app to contact people several times a day to ask what they were thinking and feeling at that moment, they discovered that we think about what is not happening almost as often as we think about what is. Significantly, thinking about what was not happening usually evoked negative rather than positive emotions. Killingsworth and Gilbert concluded that a wandering mind is not a happy mind. By being able to stay in the present, and take a curious, non-judgemental stance on thoughts, feelings, and sensations, an individual is able to step away from the battlefield they create in their brain. In becoming an observer, they can move into a position of noticing the thought or sensation. They are then able to build a distance from which new choices about behaviours and thoughts become possible.

The link with resilience

When working with clients who have lost resilience, the negative certainty with which they conceive of their future is often very strong. They want to go over events in order to look for what they could have done differently. They may hold harsh judgements about themselves and others. They will talk of limited or no choices. They believe that as intelligent adults they have applied their cognitive skills and established the truth, and that truth limits what is possible for them. Since according to Dr Annie McKee of the

Teleos Leadership Institute mindfulness 'improves cognitive flexibility, creativity and problem solving', it would seem to have a place in working with resilience issues. The UK Mental Health Foundation confirms this argument with its assertion that mindfulness changes the way people think and feel about their experiences, particularly experiences that are stressful. Similarly, renowned writer on spirituality Eckhart Tolle argues that fear, anxiety, stress, and tension are caused by too much future and not enough present, while resentment, grievance, sadness, and bitterness are caused by too much past and not enough present.

What is the evidence for the power of mindfulness?

Now that the value of mindfulness is so widely accepted, it is important to look at the evidence in the context of helping coaching clients. In his ground-breaking work developing the eight-week Mindfulness Based Stress Reduction (MBSR) programme, Kabat-Zinn found that individuals who completed the programme raised their scores on a resilience trait questionnaire. They scored higher on items related to control (a belief that they could make things happen), commitment (feeling engaged in what they were doing), and change (seeing change as a natural part of life which could also bring opportunity).

In a review of the thousands of studies that have been conducted on the value of mindfulness, the UK Mental Health Foundation concluded that people who are more mindful have a greater awareness and acceptance of their emotions and recover more quickly from bad moods. They have less negative thoughts and are able to let go of them as they arise. They hold a more stable sense of self that is less attached to external factors. They have more control over their behaviour, and are able to change their internal thoughts. In a study combining mindfulness training linked to coaching with either cognitive behavioural therapy or solution-focused approaches, the authors concluded that the choice of coaching method made no difference. The differences lay in whether the participants had or had not been offered mindfulness training in addition to individual coaching.

So what does mindfulness do to the brain?

The case for mindfulness has been enhanced by the introduction of fMRI brain scanning equipment, which has been used to study brain activity and brain patterns in people who have committed to mindfulness practices. One of the most well-known studies is that of Richard Davidson, who scanned the brains of Tibetan Buddhist monks who had between fifteen and forty years' intensive practice in meditation. Scanning showed that when meditating, the activity in their left pre-frontal cortex was far greater than in the right pre-frontal cortex to an extent never previously recorded. Since left pre-frontal cortex activity is related to feelings associated with happiness, and right pre-frontal cortex activity is associated with negative emotions and anxiety, the study suggested that one's emotions could be changed through mental training. The monks also had exceptionally high levels of gamma wave activity when meditating. Gamma waves are associated with perception and problem-solving. Davidson described them as having continuous 'aha' moments when meditating, but equally important their gamma wave activity levels continued to be high when not meditating.

As powerful as these findings are, it is important to acknowledge the level of engagement with meditation that led to those brain changes. The commitment of a Tibetan Buddhist monk to meditation is very different from that of someone not living a meditative life. A more relevant study for coaches is that of a group of workers in a bio-tech company, who after a mindfulness training programme reported feeling less stressed. A self-report, supported by fMRI scanning, showed these workers too had shifted activation levels from their right to left pre-frontal cortex. This suggests you don't have to commit to a lifetime of intense meditation to achieve such changes. Mindfulness practices at an introductory level have also been shown to increase the volume of the insula, that part of the limbic system that senses what is happening in the body. Since people experiencing stress and burnout often lose connection with what is happening in their body, mindfulness could be of value to those out of touch with the impact of stress on their body.

In the context of resilience, psychotherapist and neuroscientist Linda Graham argues that there are two neural circuits which contribute to resilience and which are developed through mindfulness. The first circuit helps focus attention and pulls the sense of self together. It provides a stable sense of self that is essential to resilience. The second is a defocusing network that allows us to link neurons in a more fluid way. This operates when we are day-dreaming, when we create a play space from which new connections emerge. This circuit helps us to be more creative when problem-solving. Both of these activities are aided by the development of the left pre-frontal cortex that comes with mindfulness practice.

As non-experts, it is easy to be seduced by studies making claims for the impact of mindfulness training on brain functioning. It is important to remember that fMRI scanning is at an early stage of development, and that claims which are attractive to coaches because they support our values and belief systems around human potential may be challenged in the future. But what has been established is neural plasticity. We now know that brain cells throughout our lives are capable of forging new connections, and that that process is the product of repeated practice. This allows us to challenge clients who suggest they are too set in their ways to learn new behaviours, but also presents the challenge that unless they are willing to commit to repeated practice they will prove themselves correct. Neuroscientists vary in their assessment of the number of repeated actions needed before a new neural circuit is created – somewhere between 17 and 64, but what is agreed is that it is frequent practice that brings about change.

One study that speaks directly to coaches to engage in mindfulness practice is that undertaken with trainee psychotherapists. Those who received mindfulness training and practised it had better client results in terms of reductions in symptoms of anxiety, anger, obsessiveness, and insecurity. This suggests that working with resilience issues in clients begins with the coach committing to their own mindfulness practice. The value of building in mindfulness practice as part of the preparation for a coaching session is that it supports you in staying focused within the session and in being able to remain emotionally detached from your own thoughts. It enhances the resilience of the coach in working with the resilience of the client.

The mindfulness caveats

As much as mindfulness has great potential when working with clients, it also has potential limitations. For some coaching clients, mindfulness will be understood as a spiritual or even a religious practice that they are uncomfortable with. They may not share the coach's enthusiasm, and fear engaging in something they associate with new age thinkers. They may have heard of it being used in the NHS and assume it is for people with mental health issues. They may dislike the term, and associate it with relaxation rather than enabling them to increase focus. They may view regular practice of mindfulness as not compatible with their busy lives, particularly if they think they need to be in a special place or sit in a certain way to practise it.

There is a difference between a structured training programme in which individuals meet regularly and are led through mindfulness practices, with set homework supported by audio recordings, and the intermittent and time-constrained contact a coach often has with clients. A coach needs to consider both how they position mindfulness with their client, and what can be achieved within a coaching relationship.

In convincing clients that there could be value in their committing to mindfulness, the positioning is important. It is useful to have a basic understanding of how the brain operates, so that you can describe some of the key functions of the brain and how they contribute to thought, emotional and sensory processes. Some authors, such as Paul Brown, Virginia Brown, and Amy Brann, have written about how the brain connects directly with coaching. With that knowledge, you can relate how a client describes him or herself when lacking resilience to the functioning of the brain. Without ever mentioning the word mindfulness, it can be introduced into coaching through a short exercise that forms part of the process for starting a session. Clients often note how it has enabled them to let go of the concerns that they were preoccupied with before the session began, and this offers an opening for discussing how else they could use the practice to sustain them when under pressure.

Case study: Introducing mindfulness

Carl is a senior manager who asked for coaching ostensibly because he wanted to gain promotion. He had never had coaching before, and when the first session began he was clearly agitated. He leapt up and down in the first few minutes, until I asked him what was happening. He said that he was uncomfortable talking about himself, and was wondering whether he really wanted to be coached. I asked him what would help him right now, and he said he just needed to calm down. We sat in silence for several minutes. When he signalled he wanted to start talking, I introduced the idea that there was something he could experiment with in the future that could help him let go of those thoughts and feelings of discomfort. We could look at it once he knew me better, and was willing to experiment. As the session progressed, it became clear that the real issue was that he had been temporarily promoted, and was struggling with standing back down. The permanently appointed boss was very different in their style, and the confidence he had gained during his temporary promotion had deserted him.

The session continued and eventually Carl asked what it was that I thought could help him, as he was aware he had feelings of panic in other situations. I offered him a short breathing exercise that he undertook readily and reported to be positive. Following this, we began and ended each session with a breathing mindfulness exercise. It helped him to focus on the 'here and now', but also to hold onto the feelings that the session had given him as he re-entered the fray. The mindfulness practice never progressed beyond that one exercise, but he saw it as resourcing him, enabling him to gain perspective and grounding him.

The importance of authenticity

The popularity of writings on mindfulness and the apparent accessibility of the exercises can make it seem as though anyone could lead a client through a mindfulness process. However, unless you have committed to mindfulness in your own practice, there are real dangers in offering mindfulness as a means of building resilience. It is like reading a book on swimming and assuming you can swim. Until you understand the impact of the exercises, the feelings they can evoke, the resistances they can stir, and the need to be supported throughout, it is irresponsible to bring mindfulness into coaching.

Case study: A cautionary tale of mindfulness

Sophie was a young manager working in a PR agency who was offered coaching as part of the company's commitment to talent development. She set herself challenging goals in terms of her development, and appeared fully committed. Shortly before her second session, her boss rang to say Sophie had received negative feedback from her direct reports and was upset. When she appeared for the session she was visibly anxious and tense. I had just been on a short course giving me my first exposure to mindfulness, and thought I saw an opportunity to apply it. I believed that a body scan exercise could help her let go of the tension, so that we could begin work. The exercise began with a focus on her breathing. Her face relaxed as she just allowed her breath to come in and out. The practice progressed with a focus on body parts beginning at her feet. When I invited her to focus on her belly, she shouted out that she could not do it and burst into tears. She became angry at being asked to focus on something that she found painful, and the rest of the session was taken up offering support. The focus on her body had reconnected her with feelings about the reasons she had left a previous job, which were linked with her inability to work with others. The current situation was making those feelings live again for her.

What did I do wrong? I had positioned the exercise as a relaxation exercise, rather than one that would heighten her awareness of sensation. I had insufficient experience to recognize the responses that even an apparently simple exercise could generate. I had not made clear that she could opt out at any stage, if she started to feel any discomfort. I had not spent long enough listening to her and the cause of her distress. I had with the best of intentions seen it as a 'fix', so that coaching could begin.

Working with mindfulness

Working with mindfulness requires that the coach be committed to its use in their own lives, as part of supporting their own resilience in working responsively with clients. Using mindfulness within a coaching relationship is constrained by the acceptance of the client, and the realities of the working relationship. With these caveats in mind, there are occasions where mindfulness can be of value in supporting client resilience. This occurs when the client is willing to commit to the idea of practice as the means by which they will increase their flexibility of thought.

There are some simple exercises you can introduce to a client and then monitor their value over the course of the coaching relationship.

Focusing on the breath

The first exercise clients are often introduced to simply focuses on the breath. The breath offers a focus for attention. Simply being asked to follow the breath gives the client somewhere to be led back to when their attention wanders into their thoughts about their daily life. Because breathing is an automatic function, which has no judgement attached to it, you cannot take a good or a bad breath. It is not possible to get it wrong. Regardless of what is happening in the head, the breath will come. Focusing on the breath shows us something we are not normally aware of – each breath is different. The realization that even as our breathing is constant it is always changing, allows us to appreciate that our thoughts are also constantly changing. For these reasons, focusing on the breath is a low-risk activity through which to introduce a client to mindfulness practice, and to enable them to experience what happens when they create the space to notice themselves.

Exercise 7.1: The mindfulness of the breath

Sit on a comfortable chair with a straight back in a place where you will not be disturbed. Place your feet flat on the floor with your legs uncrossed, allowing your back to sit a little way away from the back of the chair, if that is comfortable.

It is important that the client does not see this as an exercise in relaxation and sink into a position where they zone out of their surroundings.

Close your eyes, or if you prefer keep them open. If you choose to keep them open, soften your gaze on a point a few feet in front of you.

Some people will feel uncomfortable closing their eyes in the company of someone they do not know well, so it is important that they are given the choice.

Bring your attention to your body, starting with your feet. Explore the sensations where your feet meet the floor – the sense of touch: Does one foot sit differently on the floor than the other? Is there more pressure on one foot than the other? Notice the warmth or coolness of the foot. Does one foot or part of a foot feel warmer of cooler than the other?

It is important to signal that there are no expectations of feeling anything.

Now move your awareness up your body to the point where your body contacts the seat. Explore the sensations. Notice how you are sitting on the chair. Does your body feel balanced, or is there more pressure on one side than the other? Notice your back rising from the seat and any discomfort or tension that is present. Switch your attention to your chest and allow your shoulders to relax and soften. Become aware of your breath. Breathe normally. Do not attempt to change your breath in any way.

It is important that the client does not see this as an invitation to engage in deep breathing. You are simply inviting them to notice their breath.

Notice and follow each in-breath and each out-breath. You do not need to think about the next breath because it will just come, so focus your attention on the sensation of the breath. You may notice a sensation in your nostrils; you may notice the breaths are of different length, or that an in-breath is a different temperature to the out-breath. Just breathe. *Normalize that however they experience their breath is fine.*

Inevitably your mind will start to wander. When it does, simply gently bring your attention back to your breath. You may want to give a name to your thought: 'that's a got to do next thought', 'that's a what happened yesterday thought', and so on. Whatever thought you have, think of them as cars passing by your window. You simply notice them passing and then bring your attention back to your breath. You may notice that you are becoming bored, or that you are worrying that you are not doing it right, or that you are criticizing yourself because you can't stop thinking. Just notice the thought and gently bring your attention back to your breath.

Make sure that you allow the time for your client to experience the normal range of sensations that come when we are allowed the space to notice our minds.

There is no set time for this exercise but you may wish to experiment with allowing it to run for ten minutes.

When you feel that you are ready, start to bring movement into your body, and then open your eyes to come back into the room. Take the time you need to come back into contact with your surroundings.

There are many versions of this exercise in books on mindfulness by writers such as Michael Chaskalson, Liz Hall, and Mark Williams and Danny Penman. There are also numerous exercises to be found on the internet. You may wish to develop one that is yours. Central to the use of any exercise is that you have experienced it yourself a number of times. This will help you with the timing, the pauses and with reassuring your client as to the normality of any reaction they may have. You may wish to record it, so that your client can use it between sessions.

Common reactions to the exercise include recognition of the repetitive nature of thoughts, or of the mindlessness of many of our thoughts. Clients may be surprised that they are not being asked to stop thinking, as they assume that the aim is to create a blank space in their head. Often they report feeling more balanced and better equipped to deal with what is coming next because they feel more open. All of these reactions are valuable in helping the client to see that they can access resources for supporting their resilience through the simplicity of a breathing exercise.

The following is a development on the above and provides the client with an exercise they can do themselves without the need for any instructions.

Exercise 7.2

Explain to the client that you are going to ask them to undertake a mindfulness exercise that will only take a minute and which they will be able to do for themselves several times a day in order to stay resourced.

Sit on a comfortable chair with a straight back. Place your feet flat on the floor with your legs uncrossed, allowing your back to sit a little way away from the back of the chair, if that is comfortable.

Bring your attention to your body, starting with your feet. Notice any differences in sensation, pressure or temperature.

Now move your attention to your buttocks and notice how you are sitting on the chair. Notice any imbalance between the sides of your body. Notice any discomfort.

Notice your back and how it is resting against the chair. Notice any pain or tension.

Now bring your attention to your breath, and just breathe normally. Notice your in-breath and your out-breath. Just follow your breath.

When you are ready, we are going to count how many breaths you take in a minute. These will be just your normal breaths. Do not breathe any differently than you would normally do. When you are ready to begin, raise a finger to let me know that your minute has begun and I will then time you. All you have to do is focus on counting your breaths. This is not a test of your lung capacity. It is simply to provide you with a measure of the number of breaths you take in a 'mindful' minute.

At the end of the minute, invite the client to come back into the room, and to tell you how many breaths they took in that minute. Ask them to write it down, so that in the future they can repeat the exercise whenever a 'mindful' minute would be helpful by simply counting their minute's worth of breaths.

Case study: The mindfulness of breathing in action

Simon had been made a global leader for his company, and had come to coaching to help him develop from being an expert leader into someone who could inspire teams around the world to deliver results. He made good progress and this was commented upon in his annual appraisal. Then, shortly afterwards, the company was acquired by a competitor. His response was visceral. He shrank back into wanting to be expert. He displayed disdain for his new boss, and looked to show his superior knowledge at every opportunity. His reactions were shaped by his fear of job loss, and what he experienced as an attack on his status. He spoke of dreading the regular phone conversations with his new boss. He knew that the rage he visibly showed did not help him, but he could not see any way of stopping it.

Because I had established a strong relationship with him, and knew that he was open to experimentation if he understood the rationale for it, I suggested that he could experiment with using a mindfulness practice to prepare him for speaking with his boss.

I led him through a mindfulness of breathing exercise and asked for his feedback. He reported that he had been able to let go of the anger that he had brought into the session, and that he felt better than he had done for weeks. With this encouraging feedback, I taught him the exercise so he could do it again for himself. He accepted the scientific case for regular practice and agreed to do it twice a day for the next month. He built it into his calendar so that he would practise first thing in the morning and before any teleconference with his new boss.

A month later he reported that he had sustained the practice, and that his relationship with his boss had improved. He was now able to see that it was difficult for his boss to manage someone who they did not know, who had more subject knowledge, and who reacted aggressively to any suggestions of change.

That this exercise worked was due to the rapport we had established. I knew that he trusted me when asking him to do something that was outside of his experience. His desire for evidence before taking action was also helpful. The evidence from neuroscience was important in persuading him that it was only with practice that he would reap any benefit.

Creating mindful habits

Mindfulness is often conceived in terms of meditative exercises and the limitations of doing this within a coaching relationship have been explored. However, another dimension that can support resilience is to focus the client on dealing with their life more mindfully: that is, paying more conscious attention to how they live each day, in order to highlight how habitual and mindless we often are in our approach to living. Executives will report having no sense of whether they have eaten that day, or of what they have eaten, because they have been so focused on the next task. An individual who skips meals will have less energy available to fuel their brain functioning. They may report becoming short-tempered as the day goes on, without ever recognizing it is largely fuelled by hunger. Their resilience to deal with the demands of the job is reduced by their inability to recognize the need for the habit of eating, or of taking time away from their computer. Asking a client to develop the habit of taking time out to eat away from their desk, of being mindful what they are eating, and of noticing differences in their mood and functioning when eating different foods is a simple way of enabling them to boost their resilience. The choice between grabbing a quick sugar-release muffin or a slow sugar-release bowl of porridge en route to work is more than a choice of calories. It can influence the mood you bring to your work that day.

There are numerous mindful practices based on the principle of paying attention, including the raisin exercise, which asks individuals to allow time to experience the sight, smell, texture, and taste of one raisin, or the chocolate meditation, which offers a similar experience to those who prefer chocolate. Other exercises invite us to mindfully pay attention to daily habits, from taking a shower to walking to the station. All are designed to support a more connected engagement with the experience of living: of noticing and savouring as means by which we enhance our mood.

Breaking habits

An extension of noticing habits and being mindful in their execution is the value of breaking habits. Resilience loss is about the narrowing of thoughts, feelings, and emotions. Our habits are also about the narrowing of our choices. Some of that is helpful to daily living. Getting up at the same time each day, eating the same breakfast, going to see the type of film that we know we like, returning to the same holiday destination, all provide structure and certainty. The downside is that it can limit us. We come to believe that we can only enjoy certain types of film, or if we got up at a different time our day would be ruined. Habit breaking is about opening up the possibility that making a different choice could be rewarding, and supporting the idea that we can be flexible and can be rewarded by that flexibility.

Consider a coach who we will call Carole. She drives to her local railway station each day. She goes to the same cafe to buy her morning tea because the tea offers the strength of flavour she likes. She even sits in the same carriage. One day she discovers that she has left her phone on the charger, on a day when she has three appointments in different parts of London, two of which she has not visited previously. Her first reaction is panic followed by the instinct to drive home and be late for the first meeting. She then stops and asks herself, 'what would it be like to live a day without a phone?' What would happen if she did not receive and reply to emails, or did not text or phone home. What would it be like to try and remember the locations of buildings, or even to ask strangers for directions, rather than relying on Google Map. With that mindset of curiosity she sets out for London. She finds that when she focuses she can remember landmarks that direct her to locations. She finds that there is something enjoyable about not playing with her phone whenever she is on public transport. She rediscovers that strangers can give directions and do so with a smile. She returns home to discover that no one has noticed her lack of contact, and there is no disaster waiting in her in-box. Her mood when she returns home is light. She has enjoyed the challenge of a day without technology, because it has allowed her to access resources she had forgotten. Her resilience has been bolstered.

For people who have lost access to their resilience resources, there is often a marked narrowing of their experiences. They cling to habits as if security when they are in fact limiting the flexibility they need to access. What they need is to be helped to break habits.

Breaking a habit can be as simple as walking to work a different way, sitting in a different carriage on the train, watching a programme you assume you would not like, listening to a different radio station, not automatically choosing a sandwich at lunchtime. While the changes in habit are small, the value is in noticing the difference that a change of habit brings. Walking a different route to work helps us view our environment in a different light. Watching a different TV programme or choosing a different radio station can remind us that we often suppress some aspects of ourselves. Choosing a different lunch option can allow us to enjoy new tastes.

Exercise 7.3: Habit-breaking exercise

Invite your client to identify habits that they have created in their lives, encouraging them to explore the number of things they do each day by habit.

Ask them to consider a habit they are willing to break for a week by making a different choice, and to then reflect on the impact of breaking that habit. The new habit may relate to something they do for themselves, for example, going out into the garden to relax when they get home rather than heading for the wine bottle. It could be something they do for others, for example, calling their mother rather than waiting for her to call.

Once the client has identified the benefits of breaking that habit, encourage them to choose other habits to break.

When mindfulness is not the answer

Mindfulness is not the answer because it is popular and is being used by senior executives in FTSE companies, or even because research studies have shown that it changes the brain. It is right because you have a relationship of trust, and your client is open to exploring a different way of addressing their resilience gap. It is right when it is a genuine invitation, and wrong when it is an imposition driven by the enthusiasm of the coach. An approach that does not ask the individual to reveal anything but increases their awareness would seem unchallengeable. The value of mindfulness is linked directly to its alignment with the client's style and openness to experimentation, and the coach's skill in positioning it within the purpose of the coaching relationship.

Summary

This chapter has looked at:

- The growing body of evidence for mindfulness based on neuro-science and research studies.
- The link between mindfulness and building resilience.
- The challenges for a coach using mindfulness within a coaching contract.
- The ethics of using mindfulness exercises.
- Simple mindfulness exercises that a client could incorporate into their daily living.
- Habit noticing and habit breaking as alternate mindful practices that support the building of resilience.

8 Solution-focused coaching and resilience

My client told me in our first meeting that the cause of her difficulties was her dyslexia. When we began working together, she talked in even more detail about how her life had been blighted by dyslexia, and the failings of lecturers and employers in supporting her. When a third session began to go down the same route, I interrupted her. I acknowledged that dyslexia had undoubtedly presented difficulties, but I was also amazed at what she had achieved despite her dyslexia and others' lack of understanding. I wondered how she could use those skills to help her move forward. At first she was confused. She was so attached to her story for explaining all her setbacks that she found it difficult to look at her life in any other way. Looked at from a solution-focused perspective, it was extraordinary that she had achieved so much. She had completed a postgraduate degree, had developed strategies for managing dyslexia, and had obtained well-paid work. I suggested to her that through understanding how she achieved success, we might find clues as to what she could access to manage her way through her present tough time. From a solution-focused position, I wanted to redirect energy away from the problem and towards resources that would help her move forward. From a resilience perspective, someone who has had to deal with a significant life difficulty has resources that are of value to their current situation.

What is solution-focused coaching?

The principles of solution-focused coaching are so simple that they have an instinctive appeal, yet so simple that some coaches are sceptical of their value in working to effect sustainable change. The roots of solution-focused coaching lie in the work of a group of family therapists led by Steve de Shazer and Insoo Kim Berg. In the mid 1980s, they published a paper that to many therapists was heretical. Therapists generally started from the premise that it was through helping the client gain a deep understanding of the cause of their problem that change would occur. In contrast, de Shazer and Berg asserted that the therapist needed to acknowledge the problem but switch their interest to discovering how the client would know that the problem had been solved, and then unearthing what they were already doing that showed that they were capable of making that change. Therapists were positioned as experts in understanding the cause of client problems, and explaining that cause in terms of whichever model they had been trained in. The article suggested that therapists would be better served by seeing the client as their own expert, and the therapist as there to help the client discover their own expertise. De Shazer and his colleagues were challenging their profession to switch therapy time away from problem talk to solution talk, and to find new approaches that helped the client find their own solutions. Initial scepticism of this approach was met with research evidence that clients, who often had many years of contact with therapeutic services, were able to make sustainable change within a very few sessions: hence the initial naming of this approach as 'brief therapy'.

From the perspective of coaching, such ideas may not appear radical. Coaches position themselves as thinking partners rather than experts. Most coaches are not trained therapists and can struggle with establishing the depth to which they can appropriately engage with a client's problem. Similarly, clients are often unsure of whether coaching is therapy in disguise. For some clients this can mean fear of disclosure, whereas for others it can lead to disclosures that they later regret. Solution-focused coaching offers a framework for working with clients in a small number of sessions, giving attention to the problem, but not being fascinated by it.

The principles of solution-focused coaching

The client as expert

The principles of solution-focused coaching start from the premise that the client is the expert in their own lives. No matter how skilled or empathic the coach, they have not lived their client's life. They cannot understand the particularity of their client's situation, as it is experienced from the inside. Our role is to help the client shine a light on what their experience has told them that is helpful to moving them right now. What follows from this is that the coach's focus is on unearthing the resources the client brings rather than identifying deficits. Ask a client to tell you what they don't do well, and the words flow freely. Stop and ask them what strengths they bring to their work/life/relationships/parenting and there is often an uneasy silence as they struggle to claim skills or qualities. It is in the coach's skilful listening and questioning that those skills and qualities emerge.

Future focus

Solution-focused coaching is forward-focused. Whereas counselling and therapy look to the past for an explanation, solution-focused coaching is interested in future possibilities. How does the client want their future to be different? Rather than asking the client to explain why a relationship with a team member is poor, implicitly inviting them to create an explanation based on past incidents, or focus on failings in their own management style, the solution-focused coach is interested in how they would like the relationship to be, how they would know the relationship is improved, and centrally what evidence is already present that points to the possibility of a better relationship.

Find the exception

Solution-focused coaching is forensic in its search for information that is helpful for moving away from the problem and towards a solution. Part of that detection work is finding the exceptions to the story the individual is carrying. Once a client has constructed a problem story, they search for evidence that supports that account. In problem-focused talk, the words 'never' and 'always' are used to give additional weight to their version of the truth. The client is 'never taken seriously', is 'always overlooked', 'never does good enough work' or 'always forgets the detail'. Rather than colluding with that version, the solution-focused coach is interested in finding the exception, the time(s) when the problem did not happen, although it might have. Rather than exploring what it is like to never be taken seriously, the coach asks the client to think of a time when they were taken seriously, and focus close attention on that exception. No detail is too small or insignificant in building up a profile of the client in the exception: the clothes they were wearing, the time of day they had the conversation, where they sat in the room., and so on. By increasing the client's awareness of how they 'do' success, the coach makes available to them the resources to be successful again.

Question with simplicity

William of Ockham, a thirteenth-century monk, developed a philosophy now known as Ockam's Razor. This argues that when faced by competing hypotheses of explanation, we should start with the simplest. This principle, which sits in opposition to the human tendency to look for ever more complex (and therefore smarter) explanations, lies at the heart of the solution-focused approach. It challenges the coach to collect no more information than is needed to deal with the issue they are being faced with. It stops the coach from asking questions driven by their own curiosity, or by the need to build a complete picture of the client including their context and background. Instead, it demands that the coach ask questions that are driven by the purpose of the coaching to produce a solution. A question is positioned as a vehicle for unearthing information that is helpful to their client's thinking and from which a solution can emerge. A question is not helpful if it magnifies the problem or draws attention to the client's inadequacies. It is for this reason that solution-focused coaches do not ask 'why' questions. Instead, they ask 'what', 'where', 'how', and 'when': questions that are used purposefully to help the client find their own expertise, and to move thinking towards an outcome.

Case study: Solution-focused questioning

A client told me he felt inadequate in board meetings, because of the intellect of other board members. He was a task-focused deliverer, with a strong sales background. Those skills had secured him a director's role. Now that his brief had broadened, he had lost confidence and he found himself becoming reluctant to comment on even those areas in which he had more experience than his fellow board members. He explained his behaviour in terms of lacking the Oxbridge education the other directors had had. Rather than focusing on why he felt of less value than his colleagues, I asked him to think of a time when he had functioned well in the boardroom. He struggled to find an example, so instead I asked him to think of a time when he had interacted with a board member as an equal. He immediately described an encounter with a person who he had several times spoken of as aggressive. In the exception, he had challenged the intimidator's thinking and a better solution had emerged. A solution he had thanked my client for. When I asked my client to describe in detail how he had managed to challenge his colleague, he said that he had started by asking him questions to establish his knowledge base (rather than assuming he would know it all already), and was then able to recognize that as clever as the colleague was, he was not the expert in this instance. Once my client realized that he could deal with a fellow board member on a one-to-one basis, I asked him what he could take from that approach and transfer it to the boardroom. He quickly saw how he could operate from the stance of his right to be different but equal, and of how he could use questions to establish where he could contribute ideas rather than remaining quiet. My task then was to establish what he needed to do to keep those insights with him when he next stepped into the boardroom.

Progress comes in small steps

Models of coaching that call for the setting of large or challenging goals as the driver of motivation ignore the fact that the distance between a person's current situation and their goal can appear so great that the route to get there seems impossible. Large stretching goals work for people who have previously delivered on large stretching goals and have evidence of their own capacity to deliver, or individuals whose sense of purpose is so strong that their motivation can overcome any barrier. A client who wished to move from administration to business development was challenged that if she were to be credible, she had to show that she could bring in new business. She set herself the goal that she would bring in a sizeable contract, so that it would be impossible not to appoint her. She did this with no experience of business development. It became her purpose, and enabled her to work tirelessly outside of office hours in developing a network from which a lead could be developed. She secured the contract and got the role she wanted.

Contrast this with a person who has lost purpose. Asking them to set a big goal only heightens their sense of their own inadequacy. When a person is struggling, a progressive approach to goal achievement can be more motivating. This is the premise of the use in solution-focused coaching of scaling as a measure of achievement. Scaling is the creation of a continuum with polarities based on the client's own constructs. The client is asked to place themselves on the continuum, in terms of what they already have available to them, rather than beginning from a focus on what is missing. From this starting point, the coach then works to create movement up the scale in incremental steps of progress. With each step up, the client's sense of self-belief is increased.

Case study: Working the scale

Denise had been put into a role that she was struggling with. In a culture of monthly monitoring of performance against targets, she was visibly failing and her boss had offered her coaching as a gesture of both support and an expectation of improvement. She came to coaching with a self-image of failure, and with an admission that her instincts were to resign. As the session progressed, she used the word 'dynamic' a number of times, as a statement of how she felt the organization wanted her to be. I asked her if she would be willing to scale herself against dynamism, and asked her to define what the two polarities of dynamism would be for her.

Her dynamism continuum looked like that in Figure 8.1:

Undynamic and stuck	Dynamic and delivering
0	10
Unengaged. Doesn't contribute ideas. No show of enthusiasm.	Looks for opportunities to contribute more widely than their job spec.
Never moves away from their PC.	Links ideas and peoples.
	Operates from a mindset of possibility.

Figure 8.1   Creating a scale

O and 10 were not polar opposites but represented important constructs that Denise attached to the idea of dynamism. When asked to position herself at that moment, she put herself at 2. As a solution-focused coach, I was interested in what 'twoness' meant for her. I wanted to know what she was already using. She reluctantly identified that she was engaged at the beginning of each day, but that she became less so as the day wore on, and that she did keep in touch with her team to support them, rather than sheltering behind emails. Rather than asking her to look at what she needed to be or do in order to be at 10, I asked her in the first session to imagine being at 3. What would be different for her? She was able to visualize that if she was at 3, she would build on her boss's ideas, rather than presenting him with the reasons why they would not work (which had become her default position). This gave her a goal for the coming weeks: to signal dynamism to herself by looking to build on, rather than deconstructing, her boss's ideas.

Session by session, we took stock of where she was, noticing success and how she had achieved it, and focusing on the next step up. By the end of the sessions, she was not at 10, but she had made enough progress that she was experiencing herself as having the dynamism to deal with the demands of her role, and to keep progressing. She was also meeting her monthly targets.

Not problem phobic

A final principle is in the positioning of the problem. Solution-focused work is sometimes positioned as having a 'Pollyannerish' view of issues, where the problem is brushed aside in the desire to look only on the bright side. This was never the intention of the 'brief therapists'. Rather than the problem being avoided or dismissed, the client talks about the problem freely, but the coach listens with a focus less on the problem than on the possibility of a solution that can be found in the client's words. The coach accepts the client's view of the problem and their right to talk about it, while being focused on the possibility of change. It is the choice between listening to a client tell us about the awfulness of their situation, and wanting to understand more of that awfulness, and signalling admiration for what they are still managing to do despite the awfulness. Solution-focused work does not imply a desire to avoid the problem because it is beyond the coach's capability to sit with the difficulty, but rather a belief that the coach is of more service to the client when they help them be their own expert problem solver.

Value of the solution-focused approach to resilience coaching

The solution-focused approach links directly with a view of resilience as largely learnt through experience. It does not ask the client to learn anything new, but rather make better use of what is already there. It also allows for the idea of progress coming based on small changes. When someone is struggling with a resilience issue, the idea of being beyond the difficulty may seem unrealizable. Solution-focused work helps them to see that they are on a path, where the resources they already have allow them to keep standing and that taking small actions will help them move further along the path towards recovery. Incrementalism offers the art of the possible, when setting larger goals does not. The solution-focused approach provides a magnifying glass to help the client see what they might otherwise overlook.

The focus on resourcefulness is valuable when people are feeling stuck in a difficulty. The key to applying the solution-focused approach to resilience issues is to use the client's learning appropriately. A client who is struggling with feelings of rejection because a project they have championed has been dropped will not be convinced by being asked to think of a time when they were rejected and found a way of getting over it, if all they can call on are examples from long ago and that are unrelated to the present situation. The resources have to be ones they will trust because they are recent and relevant.

Working with the solution-focused approach

Resilience template

Because the solution-focused approach links directly with the idea of drawing on learning from similar challenges in the past, clients find it helpful to have their thinking structured, to remind them of what they already know, but have forgotten. They find it even more helpful if we can help them unpack the details of achieving success. Ask a client how they got through a period of illness, or a divorce, and the tendency to minimize will often result in generalized statements such as, 'I just got on with it' or 'What was the alternative?' There is nothing in these statements that helps the client understand the template they built at that time that helped them get through. That is where the interest of the solution-focused coach lies. What was it that enabled 'just getting on with it', and how is that model exclusively theirs?

One way of helping a client to unpack their resources is to give them a framework to bring out the colours of their resilience recovery template. Getting through can be helped by the 4 Ss: skills that the person has, supports they can call on, strategies they apply, and sagacity they can hold onto.

- *Skills* are things that the person can access at times of need. These can range from the ability to manage money really well to the ability to laugh in the face of disaster, or to keep a sense of perspective.
- *Supports* are the pit props that keep the person standing when it would be easier to fall down. These include good friends, family, a religious faith or a yoga class.
- *Strategies* are those actions that a person takes to support the goal of moving away from the feelings and thoughts associated with the present difficulty. These can include imposing a time-table on the day to prevent too much time for thinking, going to dance classes in order to have some fun time, volunteering to remind ourselves that we have things to offer to others, or having a weekly massage to release tension.
- *Sagacity* is the wisdom and insight that a person holds onto. It can come from song lyrics, novels, poetry, spiritual writings, quotes from the famous, the sayings of one's granny or learning from one's own experience.

Exercise 8.1

Before trying this exercise with clients, test it on yourself. Think of occasions when your resilience was tested. Use Figure 8.2 to focus your thinking. How did you utilize your 4 S's.

Once you have drawn up your template, look at it in the context of present difficulties. How many of those resources are you using? What have you forgotten? What is there that you might not necessarily want other people to know, but you know works for you?

Skills You drew on	Supports That kept you upright
Strategies That kept you moving	Sagacity That gave you comfort

Figure 8.2   Your resilience template

Clients find the resilience template useful, because they trust it. No matter how ridiculous it may seem to another person to listen to a particular pop song over and over again, to buy a particularly expensive chocolate or to reread a children's book, the client knows it helps them.

The power of the Miracle Question

One of the most well known parts of the solution-focused approach is the Miracle Question, which was developed by Steve de Shazer. It takes as its starting point the change that the person aspires to in order to replace the problem. Although it is phrased as a miracle, which can imply it is simply fantasy thinking, it is intended to help the person construct their desired future in the context of the issue they have brought to coaching.

The wording of the question invites the client to imagine that while sleeping a miracle happens and the client's hopes from coaching are realized. Because they are asleep they can't know that the miracle has happened. When they wake the next day, what do they notice is different about their life that tells them that the miracle has happened?

The question is designed to free up the client's thinking to imagine how their life could be different, without at this point having to do anything. In describing the picture that comes to their mind, they are designing their preferred future. Some people see this as just a backdoor way of doing goal-setting, but it does more than capture actions, it also allows for shifts in emotion.

Case study: The Miracle Question

Rachel had come for coaching because she had a poor relationship with her team. She had worked her way up from the bottom of the organization. She had moved home to gain promotions and was highly valued by her boss. However, he had fed back to her that her colleagues found her difficult to work with and a contractor had refused to extend his contract because of her. She was banjaxed by this feedback, and wanted to link this issue with her failure to have a longstanding personal relationship. This account trapped her in a story of being unlovable, and she could think of no way forward.

When she was asked the Miracle Question, she painted a picture of coming into work and people smiling at her. When asked what the smiling would give her, she answered that it would give her a sense of connection. She then noticed that she was sitting alongside the contractor, and they were talking about the issues as they developed, rather than her only being in contact with him when he presented a document that she then critiqued. She was having lunch with a colleague rather than eating alone. She was leaving on time, and going to an exercise class, and noticed that other people were still working as she left. She was going out at the weekend to buy furniture for her flat, rather than never making the time because she did not expect anyone to come to her home. Once she realized that the theme throughout this preferred future was linked to connection, the means by which she could achieve this started to flow.

We did not set goals of lunching three times a week with colleagues or leaving at 6 pm each day, as these may have been unrealistic, but instead Rachel became focused on emergent actions that moved her towards greater connection. With her preferred future in mind, she was able to apologize to the contractor for her behaviour towards him. She was more willing to give time to colleagues when they were struggling with work. She contacted old friends and invited them around to her flat, and even started volunteering at a homeless shelter. The actions she took in the service of her desire for greater connection moved her away from her perceived problem of being unlovable.

The Miracle Question in its purest form sometimes feels strange to clients. They may want to dismiss it as the stuff of fairy stories, so it is important that you find a form of words that is right for you, and which matches with your client. Hold onto the purpose of the exercise that is to help the client to define a preferred future in the context of their coaching goals. From this you can look for signs that the change is already starting to happen, and can find actions that meet the key themes of the preferred future. A particular highly cerebral client could not accept the Miracle Question in its pure form, but when I relocated it in terms of his going away for a few weeks on assignment and then coming back and noticing changes in the office, he identified shifts that captured his preferred future. When asked if there were any signs of those changes already happening, he stated a number of portents that gave him the confidence to go back and more consciously build the preferred future with his staff.

For some clients, the idea of stating a preferred future is difficult. They can only conceive the future in terms of what is not there: 'I wouldn't be crying every night', 'I wouldn't lack confidence', 'I wouldn't avoid...'. The question that then follows is: 'What would you be doing instead?' Rather than 'I wouldn't be exhausted', a client could reply: 'I would be enjoying being with the kids when they want me to play with them'. Or, 'My partner would be able to arrange for us to go out in the week rather than assuming I will only want to collapse on the sofa every night'. As soon as the client starts to focus on the 'instead', they are likely to include a future involving others and so the picture starts to build. A client who states that they will be expressing opinions at meetings instead of being 'not disengaged', has already created a new picture. The coach can now explore what others present in that meeting would notice if he were expressing opinions. The client may comment on how the others would notice that his voice is firm rather than hesitant, that he is sitting in the middle of the table rather than on the edge of the room nearest the door, or that he is leaning forward showing his desire to be 'in the fray'. Each of those comments then becomes part of the preferred future.

Unearth the exception

That there is no such thing as 'never' or 'always' is a principal tenet of solution-focused thinking. It is a challenge to the client's problem focus. It has equal value from a resilience perspective, because to live our lives according to 'never' or 'always' would be to be trapped in the rigidity that is the opposite of resilience. To never do something, regardless of the circumstances of the situation, would be to create a personal cage. Just as to conceive oneself as 'always' failing would offer no way out. When the client offers such statements with certainty, the solution-focused coach smiles inwardly, because they know there will be an exception, and that exception will be rich in useful information.

You may have noticed that by the time a client comes to you with a resilience issue, they have already started working on it. It is dangerous for the coach to see the start of the formal coaching relationship as the point at which change begins, as though coaches are alchemists. The process of wanting to see a coach is a signal that the change has started, and the client wants to speed up the process. A client who says they cannot make a decision has made a decision by coming for coaching. The person who says they have no purpose has made a statement of their will to create purpose in asking to see you. The decision to come for coaching is evidence of the exception in action. Within coaching, the search for exceptions is the seeking out of times when the problem is absent or less apparent. The coach asks the client to look for the resources they accessed within the exception, so that they can be used again. It provides appeal to clients who are sceptical of a problem-free future, because it asks them to draw on what they already know works.

Case study: Finding the exception

Chloe saw her confidence as entirely linked to how hard she worked. The rule she had created for herself was that she had to work harder than anyone else. Attempts at time management strategies were rejected, since to do less work would only lead her to lose confidence. She was about to get married and announced that she would have to take her BlackBerry with her on honeymoon. After suppressing a look of horror, I asked if she had ever been able to switch her BlackBerry off and not be worried about her confidence. She remembered a time when her mother had been hospitalized. At first, she stated that she had only switched the phone off because of the notice on the hospital wall, but eventually admitted that her work had seemed unimportant compared with her mother's needs. She remembered not switching her BlackBerry on for three days because of how tired she was when she got home. She had, however, rung her PA and asked her to allocate emails to her direct reports. When I asked her what she had done when she eventually switched her phone on, she said she had simply put the emails in a folder, and left them unread waiting to see what would happen. When I asked her about her confidence in taking such an action, she said she had been fine. Her direct reports had dealt with everything, and nothing serious happened as a result of not reading the emails. With that model available to her, she was able to go on honeymoon free of technology, and return relaxed with her confidence intact, and with a new approach to her work.

When is the solution-focused approach the right choice?

The apparent simplicity of the solution-focused approach can make it seem implausible as a means of supporting resilience, since loss of access to resilience is often linked to issues of self-worth and identity: issues that invite exploration of the cause of the difficulty. It is valid to question the evidence base for an approach that has gained popularity because of offering successful outcomes in short time frames.

The solution-focused approach has been widely used within social work as a means of supporting families by focusing on parental strengths. The case of a child killed by his parents, in which a solution-focused approach was used, led to a review by the Department of Education of the value of solution-focused working. By reviewing all of the research studies on the efficacy of the intervention, the authors concluded that the solution-focused approach is best used where clients are voluntary and there is a single-issue problem. They highlighted that solution-focused working had proved effective in supporting issues such as anxiety, depression, low self-esteem, and low self-efficacy. However, where there are multiple issues, there is a need to address the source of the problems, and this cannot be done in a short-term solution-focused intervention. Coaching is a voluntary activity, but the findings of the research caution that the coach needs to be clear in using the solution-focused approach to address resilience that the individual is functioning in other areas of their life. Where loss of resilience is a symptom of wider concerns, it is unlikely to be effective as a stand-alone approach.

Working effectively with a solution-focused approach is also strongly linked to the skills of the coach. It requires subtlety in recognizing the point at which the coach can shift attention away from the problem story, without leaving the client feeling discounted or not listened to. It requires skill in listening for resources and then being curious as to their value to the client, rather than as an immediate answer to the problem. It demands flexibility in how the techniques are used, so that they are not simply a toolkit imposed indiscriminately on the client. The least effective solution-focused coaches see the approach as a means of getting the client quickly towards an outcome, and do not allow for the resistances the client brings along the way towards a solution.

Solution-focused working is valued by clients who are tired of talking about their problem, or who have all the insight they need but are still unable move on; clients who have lost sight of their own strengths, or who cannot dare to imagine a future because it asks of them that they set goals that they believe are beyond their reach. When the coach is focused on helping the client find their solution, but is not forcing them to create one, solution-focused coaching can be an affirming process, at a time when the client feels anything but affirmed.

Summary

By looking at how the solution-focused approach can support coaches in working with resilience issues, the chapter has:

- Shown how an approach developed from a therapeutic setting has principles that sit comfortably within coaching.
- Described the principles of solution-focused working and their relevance to working with clients who are struggling with resilience issues.
- Provided exercises drawn from solution-focused principles that can be used within a coaching relationship to support the rediscovery of resilience.
- Cautioned against seeing solution-focused working as an approach for problem avoidance.

9   Positive psychology and resilience

To understand positive psychology, look no further than the life of Neil Baldwin. A former manager of Stoke City Football Club described Neil as the best signing he ever made. Keele University celebrated his contribution to student welfare with a weekend of events and the award of an honorary master's degree. He has met with princes, archbishops, and leading politicians. He has had a TV play made about his life. If you are building a picture of Neil, it will probably be wrong. Neil has significant learning difficulties. He was expected to achieve little in life, and yet has accomplished more than most of us. The secret of his success is a philosophy of life that does not see barriers. Where doctors, teachers, and social workers looked at him from a position of what he could not do, Neil operates from a position of 'What Neil wants to do, Neil does'. His attitude of positivity has enabled him to become a circus clown, to be the kit man for the football team he loves, and to create an unofficial role for himself at the local university. Inevitably, his life has had difficulty, but it is managed from a position of his belief in his right to a good life, the optimism to create it, and a strong religious faith. His life is a testimony to the power of positive psychology.

What is positive psychology?

The origins of positive psychology can be traced to the work of humanistic psychologists, such as Abraham Maslow and Carl Rogers, who focused on the human need for fulfilment and happiness. Its current prominence, however, is due to the work of Martin Seligman. In 1998, in his address as the new President of the American Psychological Association, Seligman argued that for the last half century psychologists had been consumed by an interest in mental illness. They had adopted a disease approach to their work, while ignoring the earlier mission of psychology, which was to improve normal life. Rather than focusing on the desire to be healers of the damaged, psychology should look to learn from individuals who are flourishing, and to understand what protects people from mental illness. He challenged psychologists to admit that much of the work they already did in their consulting rooms was to amplify the strengths of their patients, but this work was unacknowledged because of a mindset that saw patients as powerless.

His message struck a chord, and rapidly informed the development of a movement in understanding human experience from the perspective of the buffers that protect people. Buffers such as contentment, optimism, hope, and happiness now became the focus of attention. It has also led to a focus on understanding the strengths that people bring to their difficulties, and how positivity can support people through hard times.

Positive psychology and resilience

Resilience was an early interest of positive psychologists. While organizations focus on performance strengths, Seligman was interested in the strengths of character, and their value for dealing with difficulty. In developing the character strengths questionnaire Values in Action (VIA), Seligman challenged the accepted taxonomies of mental disorders by arguing for an equivalent taxonomy of character strengths. His six categories include emotional strengths such as perseverance and courage, interpersonal strengths such as kindness and love, temperance strengths such as self-regulation, and transcendence strengths such as gratitude, hope, and spirituality. VIA includes qualities that have consistently been identified by resilience researchers as explaining differences in coping capacity under stress, so that it is of direct relevance when working with resilience issues. The questionnaire is available online at Seligman's website, www.authentichappiness.sas.upenn.edu.

Seligman's interest in resilience also resulted in the Penn Resiliency Program. Its research concluded that based on how people talk about difficulties, they can be divided into optimists and pessimists; with the benefits of optimism for human flourishing being so great, that people need to learn to think like optimists. The resulting programme has been taught to school children and adults, but it has found its most visible outlet in a programme for over one million US soldiers. Soldiers who deal with the demands of front line duty based on a clear sense of purpose, of being supported and being connected to others often struggle with civilian life when those anchors are not present. This recognition led to the creation of a programme shaped by the principles of positive psychology. It assesses soldiers' emotional and social strengths, and then looks to develop their resilience through a focus on developing positive emotions, strengthening relationships, defining purpose, and building a sense of accomplishment. It supports this with cognitive behavioural therapy models (see Chapter 5) for challenging faulty thought patterns. In making this investment, the US Army is looking to future proof its personnel, by helping them develop their own resilience resources.

Broaden and build

While resilience is about elasticity in our thoughts, behaviours, and emotions under pressure, loss of resilience is marked by a rigidity that reduces our ability to think creatively, to see alternatives or to access a range of emotions. That recognition is the starting point for the work of Barbara Fredrickson. Her core premise is that negative emotions narrow our options, but that positive emotions do the opposite. They broaden our ideas and open our awareness to wider choices. Narrow mindsets sparked by negative emotions were valuable to our ancestors when focused on survival in a world of threat. Broadened mindsets based on positive emotions are more useful for longer time frames, because they enable us to create, to relate to others, and to plan for the future. By helping individuals broaden their positive emotional range, people can transform their lives. Fredrickson's theory of broaden and build speaks directly to the coach's task in working with those who are trapped by negative thinking. When you a help a client to notice and amplify their positive emotions, you equip them to make different choices.

Flow

When a client is struggling, it is often difficult for them to articulate strengths, although they will willingly offer up their inadequacies and self-criticisms. However, accessing strengths is vitally important to recovery. Strengths are something that come naturally to us, and in that ease the individual experiences themselves as being their real self. There is a reward in applying those strengths, because they give a sense of competence, and energy will flow towards finding those opportunities. Conversely, difficulties can mean losing access to strengths, and an unwillingness to make any claims. Positive psychology offers coaches numerous means for focusing clients' attention on what is there, if only they could notice it. Seligman's focus on character strengths is one dimension. Other writers focus on strengths as natural capacities in how we think, feel, and behave, which enable optimal functioning and performance.

Chief among these is the work of Mihalyi Csikszentmihalyi. He coined the word 'flow' to describe people operating at peak performance. He studied people in every walk of life, from surgeons to car assembly workers, to understand times when they had done their best work and concluded that there were common factors. Flow is marked by being so absorbed in a task that time passes without noticing the clock; it is the presence of a challenge that has meaning and which drives sustained and focused effort, even when the task is hard. Flow occurs when involved in tasks that offer a personally meaningful reward, whether tangible or intangible. In flow, the demands of the situation generate a positive stress which energizes us. It is what stress experts label 'eustress'. In contrast, when clients are overwhelmed by their situation they come to us with distress. All clients have a personalized flow template that they will have used time and time again to perform well, because it works for them. They are not usually aware of this, so by helping them to define their template, we provide them with something they can trust as the basis for taking action. Where clients can struggle to articulate a strength that is not captured in their organization's competency framework, recognizing their own flow pattern unearths strengths without ever mentioning the word.

Exercise 9.1: Flow exercise

Describe to your client what 'flow' is, and how to recognize it. Then ask them to identify times in their life when they have experienced it. Encourage them to think of as many examples as possible, both in and out of the work environment. Challenge them not to think in terms of their biggest achievements, but of occasions when they experienced themselves as their 'best self'. Encourage them to go back as far as they can in their life, since their current circumstances will be experienced as 'out of flow'. Support them in being honest. When feeling unhappy, a client may report they are operating out of flow all the time, so encourage them to dig deep into their life to identify moments that worked for them. Even at a difficult time, there may be flow moments present. Once they have identified a number of situations, ask them to choose three and to tell you the story of each. As they tell the story, ask the following questions:

- What attracted them to the challenge?
- What made that challenge meaningful for them?
- What support did they need in getting started?
- How were people involved in the work as they went through?
- What role did they need other people to play?
- How did they plan?

- How much freedom of action did they want?
- How did they deal with difficulties?
- How did they keep going?
- How were they rewarded?

Once your client has told you their stories, invite them to identify patterns among them. Do not push them to find connections between all three accounts, but allow them to see links that signal to them that their stories are not accidental. For some clients, talking through their stories within a session may be less helpful than being given the task as a written piece of work. Asking them to write an account of their chosen peak times, and then to reflect on the questions, can help them see patterns through reflection that they do not see in the moment. Once those patterns have emerged, invite your client to create a checklist of their flow conditions and then assess their current situation against their criteria for doing 'flow' work.

Creating a checklist is often a powerful experience, as it brings to light why the client is in difficulty. They may have taken on a role that does not match their needs, or not have available to them the kind of support they need. Their role may not be challenging in ways that are important to them, and so explains their underperformance. They may need more structure than the situation offers. With this reality check the reasons why they are not flourishing become clear.

The value of flow is that people trust it. Once they recognize that it captures truths about themselves, their motivation to move away from their current difficulty and towards their optimal conditions increases.

Case study: Trusting your flow

Melanie was furious. She had been turned down for a number of roles reporting directly to the Board, and had watched colleagues who she regarded as less able being appointed. She had challenged her boss as to why this was, and she was told that she was regarded as so rigorous in her approach that Board members did not feel comfortable with her. What began as rage against colleagues who could not accept being challenged turned to confusion. What was she supposed to do or be? Did she have to abandon who she was in order to get on? Did she need coaching to teach her how to be a chameleon? The things that she valued in herself were now being dismissed. She wavered between intellectual arrogance and crushed confidence. When we worked through the flow exercise, it became clear that she was at her best when she was dealing with difficult issues that required rigorous thinking and new solutions. She flowered when she had to challenge the status quo, and convince its defenders of the need for something different. She enjoyed being the warrior in the service of work that had integrity. She was rewarded by the difference her courage made. She was resilient under intellectual pressure. Once she owned this profile of herself, it became clear that her current organization could not offer her the conditions she needed. Instead, she sought out an organization that was visibly failing and was open to challenging how it did things. A challenge that most people would run from was exactly what met her needs, and of course when she found it, she flourished with resilience.

There are other ways of unearthing strengths. Even after completing the flow exercise, some clients doubt their own thoughts, and value the confirmation of an online self-assessment questionnaire such as Gallup's StrengthsFinder. Others accept the strengths that others see in them. You can achieve this by asking your client to identify a number of people who know them well, and then inviting their specific feedback about what they notice when your client is operating at their best. If possible, it is preferable for the feedback to be given directly to your client, rather than through the coach acting as intermediary. Asking your client to then claim the feedback they accept from an 'I' voice can be an empowering experience.

I invited a senior leader to seek out feedback because his account of himself was highly self-critical, and he doubted himself. He felt he was making no impact despite working excessively hard. When he asked his team what they noticed about him when he was at his best, they told him they valued his listening skills and understanding of individuals, which enabled everyone to contribute without fear. They valued his subject expertise, which he used to make sound decisions, and his honesty, which meant he did not shy away from the difficult. They recognized his strong sense of purpose, which meant he gave a great deal of himself to his work, and his perseverance in sticking with issues until they were resolved. When he spoke those words from his own voice, he cried. He was touched by their ability to see in him qualities that were central to how he lived his life and approached his work. Their recognition of who he was gave him the confidence to continue working authentically.

Alex Linley, a leading positive psychologist talks of strength spotting: of finding means to help the client spot their own strengths. As a coach you can do that by asking questions that take a 360-degree view of strengths. The mnemonic REFLECT is one I developed to help me remember key indicators of individual strengths.

Real: When do they feel most themselves? When are they really comfortable?

Energy: When are they energized by what they are doing, so they want more of it? When do they notice their voice becomes more passionate?

Focus: What do they notice about the things which attract their attention? What does that highlight about their motivations?

Learning: What do they enjoy learning about?

Ease: What do they notice comes more easily to them than other people?

Childhood memories: Which of their childhood interests continues to engage them as an adult?

To do: What things always get done first on the 'to do' list and which things never get done? What does that tell them about their natural strengths?

Positivity

If unearthing and building on strengths is one pillar of positive psychology, then a second is positivity and in particular the work of Barbara Fredrickson. Her broaden and build theory is based on two premises: that positive emotions open hearts and minds and make people more creative and receptive, and that positivity transforms us for the better because it enables us to build new skills and knowledge. Her claims are informed by her scientific research. In one study, the link between positivity and resilience was established by asking participants to complete a resiliency scale questionnaire, and to track their emotional ups and downs over a month before recompleting the questionnaire. The findings showed that those who reported more positive emotions grew their resilience over the month. Similarly, in studying reactions to 9/11 in the weeks immediately following the attack, Fredrickson showed that those who scored higher on a resilience questionnaire experienced more positive emotions such as empathy, love, and gratitude than participants with lower scores. It was not that the more resilient did not experience negative emotions such as fear and anger, but that they were able to intersperse them with other emotions.

The finding that positivity is not about eliminating negative emotions but about increasing the presence of positive ones is at the heart of Fredrickson's work, and in particular the conclusion that a positivity rating of 3:1 is necessary for flourishing. A ratio of 3:1 has also been claimed by Marcial Losada, a mathematician who studied boardroom behaviour and correlated it with business performance. Boards who made positive statements, who focused their inputs on others rather than themselves, and made statements of enquiry rather than advocacy on a 3:1 basis were better business performers. His explanation for difference was that more positive Boards were able to remain flexible when faced by challenge. It seems that organizational resilience as much as individual resilience is helped by positivity.

Creativity

The claim that a broadened mindset increases creativity has also been evidenced in scientific studies. One study by Toronto University showed that participants who had been influenced into a positive mindset through playing upbeat music had greater peripheral vision. Because they were feeling positive, they noticed more of what was around them. Their vision widened. They were also more verbally creative than a group who had been played music to induce a negative mindset. Taken outside of a laboratory setting, their findings suggest that people who have more positivity in their lives are more able to deal with adversity in an open-minded way, because they see more solutions.

Case study: Positivity and creativity

Karen had had a stellar career as the CEO of a charity when she was diagnosed with an aggressive form of cancer. It took her away from her role for over a year. When she recovered and returned to work, she asked for coaching. A year is a long time in the life of an organization. The agenda had shifted; colleagues had taken over parts of her role and were anxious to hold onto them. It would have been easy for her to feel negative about her team, to fight for territory or to lose confidence in herself. Instead, she accepted what had changed, including herself, and rather than being caught in negative emotions, she focused on who she now wanted to be. She created an image of a champagne bottle fizzing with bubbles to signal that she wanted to be energized by challenge, rather than simply grateful for having returned to work or resentful of others. With that image she was able to start tracking what made her fizz and what left her flat. By noticing her fizz, she started to redirect her energies towards those things that energized her thoughts and emotions. The champagne image enabled her to look more broadly and not to define herself as a cancer patient in remission. It enabled her to move into a new CEO role that she would never have imagined prior to her illness.

Working with positivity

The challenge in working with clients to increase their positivity is the oppositional power of negative thinking. Because negativity had a survival value for our ancestors, it is a natural place to revert to when feeling in danger. Because we experience negative emotions intensely, we have a negativity bias. We notice negative emotions more readily, whereas positive emotions can slip us by. Our role is to help our clients pay greater attention to the multitude of positive emotions that are experienced in the course of a day, but because they are on a small scale their potential benefits are ignored. The pleasure felt in listening to a toddler in the train carriage happily chatting to its parent can be quickly lost in the feelings of frustration at the train's late arrival.

For a client to start moving towards a 3:1 ratio, when their own self-assessment is often the reverse, they need to start noticing themselves. You could ask your client to complete the checklist shown in Figure 9.1 every day for a week. The first column asks the client to report the emotions they were most aware of accessing. This may feed into their negativity bias, as they remember the day as being overwhelming and defined by their annoyance at an action of a friend or partner. The second column invites them to revisit the day and to recognize what else they experienced that they may not have acknowledged initially. This allows to be noticed those small emotions that were also present, but did not sing out so loudly: laughing with a colleague, the enjoyment of reading a story to their child, or their appreciation of having dinner cooked for them. As important as logging the ratios over time is understanding what results in a better or worse ratio. What were they doing on a day when their positivity ratio was higher that offers clues as to what they need to do more of?

No individual day's rating will be significant, so it is important that your client completes it over a period of time. You may wish to turn it into a spreadsheet rather than a paper version. Alternatively, by logging onto Barbara Fredrickson's website (www.positivityratio.com) individuals can keep a record of their positivity. In completing the checklist, it is important to accept the client's assessment of an emotion, rather than judging an emotion as positive or negative. A client who reports they mostly felt angry, may have used that anger on themselves or it may have galvanized them into action. Experiencing disgust may have motivated them to speak out rather than remain quiet. Equally important is knowledge of what explains their rating, as it enables them to see that they do have control over how they feel. Rather than seeing themselves as the victim of their emotions, they can start to notice that actions they take have an impact on their positivity ratio. By increasing awareness of their emotional range, they can experience the benefit of having those emotions available to them.

In reviewing today, which of the following emotions have you experienced?		
Emotion	**1. Tick those emotions which you have experienced *most* today**	**2. Tick those which you have experienced at *some point* during the day**
Afraid		
Amazed		
Amused		
Angry		
Annoyed		
Appreciated		
Ashamed		
Awe		
Close		
Confident		
Contemptuous		
Content		
Curious		
Cynical		
Disgusted		
Enjoyment		
Gratitude		
Guilt		
Happiness		
Hope		
Inspired		
Interested		
Irritated		
Jealous		
Optimistic		
Overwhelmed		
Peaceful		
Proud		
Sad		
Scared		
Sceptical		
Self-blame		
Self-conscious		
Shame		
Stressed		
Stupidity		
Suspicious		
Thankful		
Trusting		
Unhappy		
Weary		
Positive:Negative Ratio **Combine both columns' totals to obtain the overall ratio**		
What explains your ratio?		

Figure 9.1 The Positivity Ratio Checklist

When a client is unable to distinguish beyond broad emotions of unhappiness or stress, you can become more granular and invite them to create a day in detail from the moment they got up to the moment they went to bed, all the while logging activities and how they felt, in order to help them recognise that within their unhappiness or stress they were accessing other emotions that could be of value to them.

Before offering these exercises to a client, try them out yourself. You will likely discover that you too do not consistently have a 3:1 ratio. Research suggests most people are nearer to a ratio of 2:1. However, for our own and our clients' healthy flourishing, a 3:1 ratio is the goal. When a client consistently reports a ratio less than 1:1 with little variation across days, it may be an indicator of clinical depression, and your role then becomes one of supporting them in finding specialist help, rather than continuing with the exercise in the hope of improving the ratio.

Too much positivity?

Critics of positive psychology sometimes interpret the 3:1 ratio as 3:0. This is not the intention. Simply focusing on the positives does not allow recognition that sometimes there are real constraints that justify negativity. Only focusing on positives makes our clients like a balloon that becomes so overinflated that it pulls away from the hand holding the string. They become ungrounded. It is through acknowledging but not becoming overwhelmed by negatives that positives can be worked with. Negativity that is appropriate and specific is helpful, just as positivity that denies truth is not. Finding the right relationship between the two is like driving a car. Positivity is the accelerator that moves the car forward, but recognizing when to apply the brake ensures the car handles the bend in the road. The focus on positives at a time of difficulty is valuable because it helps the client to remove their foot from the brake.

To be helpful, positivity has to be genuine. Clients should not be shoehorned into positivity. Being told 'don't worry, be happy' simply annoys. Positivity does not deny the reality of negative emotions. It seeks instead to reduce over-zealous negativity, because when people are in a difficult situation they may become forensic when searching for additional data to support their story. They overblow the trivial, or ruminate on events so that the implications for their future become bleaker. They can create a cycle of negative thoughts fuelling negative emotions, fuelling more negative thoughts. This process has no useful purpose in resolving their difficulty, and corrodes counterbalancing emotions. There is the difference between necessary negativity, which can enable us to face the facts, and excessive negativity, which keeps us stuck. It is appropriate for a client to feel sadness or anger or disappointment when a hoped for outcome does not arise. It reflects the importance they attached to that goal, but if those emotions continue and blight the vision of any other possibility, they risk becoming like Miss Havisham, trapped in her wedding dress decades after being jilted and unable to move on. The aim in coaching from a positive psychology perspective is not to eliminate negativity but to give it its right size.

Case study: Working with the negative in a positive way

Raj is a logical, analytical, highly intelligent professional. All of that left him when he was told his performance at a senior level meeting had not gone well. When I met him, he rejected the feedback he had been given and discounted those who said they had experienced him as arrogant, but he also saw his future as bleak. He felt lost. How could he work for a company that did not rate him? Why would anyone else want him? Every attempt to get him to open up his thinking was met with a counterargument of the hopelessness of his situation. At a loss as to how to get him to broaden his attention, I engaged him in a strengths exercise, as a means of allowing him to acknowledge what he did bring to his work. I then asked him to consider the feedback in the light of his strengths. With a different basis from which to look at himself, he saw that his love of forcefully arguing his case had not played out well because when he became passionate he disconnected from the impact he was having. The need was not to lose his passion and love of argument, but to develop his emotional intelligence to allow him to know when to change his stance.

Gratitude

An additional perspective to noticing positive emotions is to be able to notice what is okay in the middle of what is not okay. Gratitude has a place in positive psychology practice because by noticing what we have reason to be grateful for, our satisfaction increases. Asking clients to stop each evening and notice what they have cause to give thanks for can help clients connect to a larger purpose. They are encouraged to move attention away from their immediate concern and to notice what else is happening in their world. To notice what their children or partner has brought into their life that day, to appreciate their health, to notice what pleasure they got from walking the dog in the park, or to acknowledge the value of their faith in sustaining them – all are gifts. Gratitude can be seen as a secular form of prayer; a place to acknowledge what is good in our lives.

Inviting clients to identify three things each day to be grateful for can seem a big ask. At first they may simply interact at the level of 'I am grateful I got through another day', and need to be challenged to think of themselves as a whole person rather than as fulfilling one particular role. At first, it may only be possible for them to find one thing a day to be grateful for. With practice, the size of the gratitude lens widens, and as it does so the ability to notice the small things that make up the texture of life grows, along with the pleasure they give. As a coach, be curious as to what the client is grateful for, as it will reveal those things that are important to them. They are likely to link to key motivators of autonomy, connection, purpose, and competence. At a time when their loss of resilience may be linked to one of those themes, recognizing that their needs can be met in small ways provides a support to their recovery.

When is positive psychology the right choice?

A strong case has been made for positive psychology in helping people access resources that are known to aid resilience. However, a relentless use of positive psychology is never the right choice if it denies the legitimacy of negativity, or the reality of a client's situation. Positive psychology has been criticized for denying the context that the client is working within. The 'if you can dream it, you can achieve it' school of positivity denies the possibility that an individual's circumstances can be proscribed by educational, financial, social or health limitations. Acknowledging those realities does not remove the value of focusing on strengths and positivity, but counsels that the conversation needs to work with those realities. Similarly, a client will not engage with the tools of positive psychology until they feel their story has been heard and understood, or they are weary of being caught by their own negativity but cannot find a way out.

Summary

In looking at the role of positive psychology in working with resilience issues, the chapter has:

- Described the work of key thinkers on the development of positive psychology.
- Offered a number of ways of helping clients to access strengths when they are caught by their deficiencies.
- Positioned positivity as a research-led ally in helping clients to move forward from a setback.
- Offered means by which coaches can help clients access positive emotions and positive experiences that will support them in broadening their perspective.
- Presented means of balancing negativity with positivity without denying the role of the negative.

10 Coaching for career resilience

The face smiles out from the recruitment poster. It reads, 'I have a stable job in an unstable world'. The message is clear, the employee's happiness is based on his ability to have beaten the odds and found security in an insecure labour market. He has achieved what many career coaching clients bring to their sessions: the hope that the coach can help them find stability and certainty. That desire shifts what they expect of the coaching relationship. Where a client will accept coaching as a non-directive thinking space to address issues around their leadership, that same person when they confront a career issue will want the coach to offer knowledge, advice, tips, and expertise, in order that their career recovers from setback or disappointment. The challenge for the coach is whether to meet that expectation, and position themselves as career expert, or help the client to develop career resilience skills for managing themselves going forward in a world of uncertainty.

It is clear that the context of careers has changed. The labour market our clients work within is shaped by the speed of technological innovation and communication. Organizations are constantly restructuring, and as they do so career paths become well hidden or torn apart. Work has become globalized, so that there are no guarantees that skills are not replicable for less cost in another part of the world. The reputation of an organization can be trounced through high-profile events that reduce individual marketability. Strategies are constantly changing, which has an impact on which skill sets are valued. Economic downturn and legislative changes mean plans for retirement are rewritten and the individual has to find ways of reconnecting with work, at a time when they hoped to disconnect. One thing that has not changed is the expectation from employees that organizations should offer career certainties. A CIPD (2014b) report on employee trends found that 33 per cent of employees feel their career has failed to meet their expectations, and a quarter are dissatisfied with the level of career development offered.

It is human to want control over our working lives and to be disturbed when it is taken away. It is why approaches to career development that hold the promise of easy answers are attractive. It is why clients look to career coaching to give them those answers: to tell them what they should be doing, and to show them how to guarantee success. In looking for that certainty, clients experience a disconnect between what they have experienced in their own lives and what they expect of their career. If you ask a client to review their life experience and to assess how much of it has been lived to a plan, whether in their career or their personal life, the answer is generally that their life has been largely shaped by opportunity and chance. However, when they seek career coaching they are often seeking a predictable planned future. The language of careers encourages this idea. People will talk of career ladders, or a career path: structures that offer a clear route and steps to be taken. The word 'career' derives from the French word for racecourse, which implies that you can at least know where you are in the race, and compete to win it. This language clashes with the reality that most careers are based on shift and change. One study that followed a group of 170 people for twenty-five years found that two-thirds experienced changes in their original occupational choice. There are no career certainties.

One reason why individuals whose own lived careers tell them that working life is unpredictable and shaped by context, still deny this reality can be laid at the feet of two men whose career theories dominated the twentieth century: Frank Parsons and Donald Super.

Fit the person to the job

Frank Parsons established the Vocational Bureau in 1905 to help people make better work choices. Rather than people simply doing whatever work was available, he developed a matching approach, which stated that individuals needed to know what their abilities and interests are, and to have information on the demands of occupations. Know what you are good at and interested in, find a job that offers those qualities, and you have a perfect match that will shape the rest of your working life. The logic of this approach has had a powerful impact on how careers coaching developed. What Parsons' model assumed was that people did not change, and neither did the demands of jobs. The model worked for part of the twentieth century because it matched with social patterns that valued security. It also worked for organizations, because the extension of the person-fit model was that if people were in the right job, they would perform better, would be happy, and would stay.

Parsons' influence can be seen in career psychometrics designed to help people find the right job, based on matching interests and skills with the characteristics of occupations. The underlying assumption was that once found, the choice would shape the rest of their career. Clients continue to bring this assumption to career sessions, where they talk of never having found the right career, as though there is one elusive job 'out there' that they were meant to do, if only they could identify it.

Career development theory

Donald Super came to careers theory half a century after Parsons, and he looked at careers from a broader perspective. Rather than careers work being about helping individuals to find the right job that matched with their interests, abilities, and skills, Super viewed individuals as having different needs from their work over their lifespan. Those needs could be predicted by their age. Aged 15–24, individuals are exploring their career. They are trying out jobs, and discovering who they are in relation to work. Mistakes are allowed at this stage. By 25, they will have made a decision, and the focus shifts to establishing their skills and identity within that work. These are the career growing years when the person is also establishing their identity as a partner and parent, and the work is of career progression. By the mid-forties, individuals are in a maintenance stage and accept what they have and look to hold onto it. By 65, individuals have reduced their output and are ready to retire.

From the vantage point of the twenty-first century, Super's model makes little sense. It takes no account of women's different experience of career or the complexity of lives. It does not reflect the years of exploration that many young adults now have to accept before they establish any stability in their working lives. The idea of maintenance and simply being able to enjoy and hold onto what one has achieved is not how many middle-aged clients experience their working lives. However, despite the paucity of the model for twenty-first-century living, it continues to have a hold. Clients still believe that there is an age-stage model that predicts where they should be in their career, and they make a judgement as to whether they are behind or on track. They still largely see exploration as an early career need and the sign of being an adult as committing to one line of work. They still hope that careers can be plotted ahead. These beliefs hold despite the evidence that certainties in social patterns of behaviour and the working of the labour market no longer hold true.

Parsons' and Super's theories were fine for the last century, particularly if you were a well-educated man, working in a large successful corporate environment, and with conventional life patterns. They do not work in the twenty-first century. We need new theories and two have emerged that are of value in helping our clients be career resilient: career constructivism and chaos theory.

Career constructivism

Constructivism is the way in which we create meaning. Chapter 3 highlighted that we carry stories that shape how we respond to events, and that it is in understanding those stories from new perspectives that we create new ones. The career theorist Mark Savickas invites us to work with the multiple stories clients hold about themselves, and to look for life themes that are relevant for guiding work choices. Those themes are revealed in personally significant stories where people have used meaning, rather than pure logic, as the basis for making decisions. It is in helping people to understand their own stories that coaches equip clients to be able to take actions and to adapt themselves to circumstances, enabling them to trust what they know to be true. Career coaching shifts from matching people to roles, to helping clients use their life themes to make good choices. In the chapter on narrative you were invited to work with one significant story that marked the client's loss of resilience, in order to unearth the identity they were carrying with them. Career constructivism is interested in many stories going back to childhood. In a career coaching session, the coach asks questions such as:

- Who did you admire when growing up? What did you admire about them?
- What are the books you remember from childhood? What made those books important to you?
- What were the TV programmes you always watched? What did you connect with in those programmes?
- What is your favourite film? Tell me the story. What is it that makes it memorable for you?
- Do you have a saying, or a line from a poem, film or song, that you refer to in how you live your life?

In their answers, clients reveal key themes about what influences their living, which is augmented by asking them to tell stories about key events in their career. This is a process that enables clients to see the degree to which there is connect or disconnect between their life themes and their living of their career.

Case study: Career constructivism

When asked the above questions, Lynne told me of her admiration for her mother who had been a single divorced parent, who worked hard all her life, and who remained optimistic and curious into old age. She remembered from her childhood loving stories about independent girls who took risks, and a favourite comic book character – a girl who helped the Dutch resistance in the Second World War. She loved TV programmes and documentaries that focused on injustice, and longed to be Robin Hood rather than Maid Marion. Her favourite film was 'Schindler's List', as it showed that humanity exists within inhumanity and that humanity can cause people to act in extraordinary ways. She remembered the line from the film 'he who saves one life saves the world', and she used it to enable her to look for what she could do to help others. She readily recognized her life themes. When she put them alongside her career story, she could see that while the themes had directed her towards a career in helping others, she had abandoned her career control in allowing others to tell her what was right for her, and staying in roles far too long because of hoping it would bring security, and then discovering it did not. She had stopped being curious.

By constructing her life themes, she was able to really connect with who she was, rather than who she thought she needed to be within work. She could see that trusting her life themes allowed her more freedom of action, as they positioned her as autonomous rather than dependent. It provided a starting point for considering what she would do differently if she operated from those themes. It confirmed that her career choice was not accidental, and it enabled her to trust that by taking risks she would become more of who she was.

Criticism of constructivism

Career constructivism is an empowering way of working with clients. It enables them to trust their own self-knowledge. A criticism is that it does not address context. It does not challenge the client to consider issues of ability or the reality of constraints. It can exaggerate the degree of control that a person has over their career options by simply looking at that individual's perspective. The truth is that individuals sit within systems. The individual experience is just one doll within a much larger babushka doll. Surrounding the individual is another encapsulating the immediate system of their gender, ethnicity, sexual orientation, their health, knowledge, and education. That sits within a larger social system of their family, work, and community, which in turns sits within an even larger economic-societal system incorporating globalization, socio-economic status, geography, and employment markets. Resilience can only be actualized if there is an acknowledgement that careers are not linear and predictable, and that unpredictability comes from the wider context. Careers work needs a larger theory and here chaos theory has a role.

Chaos theory

The idea that a butterfly flapping its wings in China can cause a meteorological disaster on the other side of the world is widely used as a descriptor of the unpredictability of life. The image comes from the work of Edward Lorenz, an experimental meteorologist who predicted weather using computer models. One night he approximated some data and then left the computer to run. When he returned in the morning he discovered that the results diverged from previous data to a much greater degree than his approximation would have predicted, and that the longer the programme ran the greater the divergence became. Lorenz came to realize that very small changes in complex systems have the potential to transform a system in unexpected ways. He saw that there is not a linear relationship between the size of the change and the impact it can have. In business, it is seen in how the decision made in one part of the world to open or close a plant in another part of the world transforms the local economy and the life chances of local workers. The decision of a journalist to hack into the voicemail messages of a missing schoolgirl leads to the closure of a 168-year-old newspaper. The external appointment of a new CEO impacts on the career expectations of a generation of leaders. In science, chaos theory has challenged thinking prevalent since the Renaissance, that there are fixed laws. It allows for the admission of chance and contingency. In working with career issues, it cautions that outcomes cannot be controlled, and that our clients need to learn how to live with uncertainty in order to work with its possibilities. Chaos theory does not simply give up the idea of control, but rather it asks that there is a need for both adaptation to the dynamism of the system, and a need for resilience in order to maintain stability in the face of change. It is what is asked of engineering structures: a tower needs to have sufficient adaptability that it can move slightly in response to weather conditions, but also needs to be able to return to a position of stable strength. In working with resilience issues in a career context, issues of stability and flexibility are equally important.

The flex-stability ratio

When making a career choice, we are defining ourselves. If a person chose to become an accountant, it does not mean they could not have done many other things. They may only become aware of that possibility when they come in later years to trust their self-knowledge rather than that of parents or teachers. In exploring with them their choice options, the coach is interested in how rigid or flexible the individual is, so that they can understand their boundaries for change. The coach is equally interested in where stability is important to them, so that the relationship between the two can be explored. In my years working as a careers counsellor within an art school, I was regularly contacted by successful professionals who believed their lives would be a lot happier if they were artists. My role was to enable them to gauge their flex-stability ratio, so that they could assess if they had sufficient stability of purpose and identity to sustain them if they extended their boundaries into a world with few certainties.

Working with chance

Career books have contributed to the belief that good careers are planned, and lack of planning contributes to failure to achieve potential. Fail to plan means plan to fail. The fact that this does not reflect what people see around them does not reduce the belief that planning is important. What chaos theory tells us is that chance is a key part of how the universe operates, and the need is to be alert to chance and work with it. It is in grabbing the unplanned and unforeseen that significant change occurs. It is the central premise of the film 'Sliding Doors'. In one version, the female character just gets through the tube carriage doors before they close; in the other, the doors close before she can get on-board. Both those actions, divided by no more than a few seconds, led to distinctly different outcomes. There is no right or wrong outcome – they are just different.

Our clients have been sold a career model built on rational messages: that hard work will attract reward, that a successful career is one of steady progression within an area chosen in early adulthood, that investing in an MBA will increase earnings and career outcomes exponentially. They are then angry, confused or defeated by the discovery that careers are often shaped by chance events and there are few certainties. In order to work with these truths, they need to connect with their core stability in order that they can work with what is, rather than what they would wish. It is here that chaos theory has an explicit link with resilience, since the qualities which career chaos theorists Robert Pryor and Jim Bright identify as providing that stability are the ones that underpin resilience: optimism, flexibility, self-belief, persistence, and purpose.

Tolerance for change

Some clients seek career coaching because they want change, whereas others seek it in order to minimize any change. They want the world to meet their expectations and hope the coach has labour market knowledge which they lack, or they want to discover how to change their boss's perception of them so that they get the career outcome they believe they are due. They can see change happening around them, and they don't want it. The coach's task is to support their resilience so that they can work with deviations from the expected.

Case study: Career growth through uncertainty

When I met Alastair he was on the main board of a UK bank. He did not look or sound like other board directors I had met, so I was curious as to how his career had led him to the top of the organization. His story was of joining the bank at 16 and building his career in a slow and steady predictable way. By his forties, he was in a middle management role and according to career theory was moving into his maintenance stage. Then the bank was taken over, change went viral, and he saw senior colleagues freezing in panic or defending the status quo. He chose another route. He decided that this was his career chance moment. He saw there was a lot of new work to be done, and while he did not know any more than his colleagues about how it could be done, he brought his optimism and open-mindedness to the challenge. That response became his career catapult, and within a short time he had outstripped colleagues who had once managed him. He admitted he was no more able than they were, but he had seen opportunity where they saw loss.

How do coaches increase a client's openness to change?

In helping our clients develop an openness to change, many of the approaches offered in previous chapters are relevant: positive psychology helps people recognize strengths that will help them deal with the change; solution-focused coaching enables them to deconstruct how they have dealt effectively with other changes in their life; cognitive behavioural coaching helps clients to challenge their own thought processes; and mindfulness can equip them to stand apart from what they are attaching to the change. However, there are other approaches specific to careers work that are of value.

Career resilience

The concept of career resilience was first articulated in the 1990s by writers who recognized that the old certainties that had marked the careers of the successful were breaking down. The response of those writers was to want to help people protect their careers by learning skills that would give them an advantage in the labour market. They warned readers to break away from the idea that the organization would look after their career, and to see themselves as an independent resource, 'Me plc', engaged in a transactional exchange of skill for reward. The career-smart should let go of old ideas of reward for commitment. In order to sustain marketability, they should ensure that they constantly developed their skills. They should network inside and outside their organization, and build a visible profile. They should build relationships with key stakeholders. They should be associated with work that was of high value to the organization, and distance themselves from work that was of declining value or linked to failure. They should project self-confidence, even if they did not feel it. They should construct a strong brand. Career resilience was a set of things to be done. However, the drawback as I regularly discovered in career coaching sessions was that clients could only do those things if they were feeling resilient. Once a person feels resilient, those actions make perfect sense and flow easily. Without resilience, they seemed undoable. The thought of going to a social event with a networking agenda, of promoting themselves to a senior leader or creating a brand filled them with horror. The doing of resilience is based on the being of resilience. Until the being is addressed, the doing is unlikely to happen.

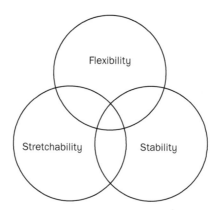

Figure 10.1   The Career Resilience Model

In response to this, I looked to clients who had worked through career difficulties and examined how they had weathered those storms and moved on to make their careers work for them. From this I developed a Career Resilience Model which captures the two themes of career chaos theory – the ability to flex in response to change, and the ability to utilize areas of stability – and added a third: the ability to stretch beyond one's expected boundaries. That relationship is shown in Figure 10.1.

Flexibility

Elasticity is the core element of resilience. In careers coaching, flexibility encompasses an ability to acknowledge change in the business environment, but also changes that individuals have managed within their own lives.

Flexing to the external world

When clients seek out coaches, they are often baulking at a change that has had a particular impact on them. The reality is that they will have already dealt with a number of changes. Inviting them to recognize the degree of business change they have already been exposed to helps them to realize that it is not change itself, but this particular event, that is significant for them. That can provide a useful opening for understanding what this particular change means for their sense of self.

When a client is worried about their future, and is seeking the reassurance of stability, offering them a framework for acknowledging possible future change is a starting point for challenging the idea that coaching or the business environment can offer stability. It begins the process of positioning resilience as the ability to work with shift.

Many strategy models exist but a simple one to use in a careers context is PESTLE: a model frequently used for business planning. Asking a client to work through the framework equips them to begin assessing their career against that emerging picture.

In discussing their PESTLE analysis, a client is likely to recognize the difficulty of predicting the future, and which element of their scenario planning will have most impact. Rather than that being a reason for not looking ahead, focus their attention on probability, and its meaning for their future career. Does it highlight some certainties that they would be foolish to ignore? For example, in working with a mobile phone manufacturer some years ago, their analysis of social and technological changes highlighted that the future of competitive success was not in design alone but also entertainment content. Ambitious individuals needed to find ways of getting involved in what was then a small area of

Table 10.1   PESTLE your career

Strategic perspective	Impact on my sector	Impact on my organization	Possible meaning for my career
Political National or international issues			
Economic Macro or micro enconomic factors			
Social Social changes in how lives are being lived			
Technological What is being brought into the organization, or is affecting how people live their lives			
Legal Changes that could affect how business is done			
Environmental Regulations Location of work			

the business, if they were to align with the emerging future. It also highlighted that demand would reach saturation point in developed countries, but there were potential growth areas in parts of the world with no history of landlines. Their requirements of mobile phones would be very different from those of developed countries. Suddenly, countries that had hitherto been of little interest in career terms became avenues for career progression.

Personal flexibility

Flexibility is also about recognizing one's own capacity for working with the unexpected based on life experience. The butterfly has become a motif for chaos theory, and career researcher Tony Borg has developed a butterfly model to enable individuals to acknowledge the relationship between the planned and unplanned in their life. The model is shown in Figure 10.2.

When clients acknowledge what has been planned and unplanned in their lives, it allows for the recognition of how much or little of their life

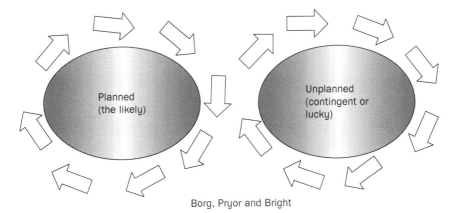

Borg, Pryor and Bright

Figure 10.2 The Career Butterfly Model (Reproduced with permission from Borg, T., Bright, J.E.H. and Pryor, R.G.L. (2006) The Butterfly Model of careers: illustrating how planning and chance can be integrated into the careers of high school students, *Australian Journal of Career Development*, 15 (3): 53–8)

has rested on planning, but also the resources they brought to dealing with the unplanned. It enables recognition that some of those things that were planned were not necessarily their best choices, and that good things can come from the unplanned and the unwelcome.

Inviting your client to look at their working life as a butterfly that requires both wings in order to move, enables them to acknowledge what of the unplanned is of continuing value to them in dealing with both what is happening to them right now, and for the future. Figure 10.3 provides an example of the career butterfly model in use.

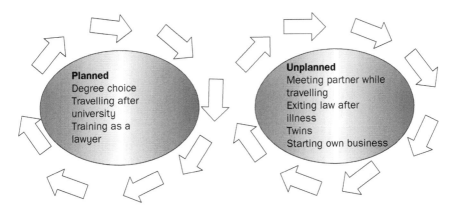

Figure 10.3 The Career Butterfly in Action

Stability

Stability is provided by those things which the client knows to be true. It encompasses the identification of performance and character strengths as identified in Chapter 9. It also encompasses purpose and meaning. Purpose is a key supporter of resilience. It helps people to persist when things are difficult, and provides an anchor for the choices they make. Clients can see purpose as linked to career goals: my career will have meaning when I am a Board member, have secured my financial future or have produced something which lasts. Once those goals are reached, purpose is lost, unless it is linked to something that transcends particular goals. Purpose encompasses the big questions of 'who am I' and 'what am I here for?' Those questions can be difficult to answer. When a client is struggling with the notion that they attach any purpose or meaning to their work, then using an exercise like The Five Whys can help them find an anchor.

Exercise 10.1

Invite your client to write down a one-sentence answer to the question:
Why do you go to work?
Having written the answer, ask them to answer the question:
Why do you want to do that?
Having written the answer to that question, invite them to answer again:
Why do you want to do that?
Repeat the question until the question 'why?' does not elicit any further thought. This usually takes 4–6 responses. Invite them to share with you what their answers have highlighted for them about their purpose.

The exercise can be done verbally, but writing answers encourages the client to reflect without censoring before speaking.

Case study: The Five Whys

Sean had been far more successful than he had ever expected, and he came to coaching because he said he no longer had the motivation to work. He was only in his forties and he had no thoughts about giving up work. He had a business that was doing fine, but he had no motivation to do anything with it. He also felt embarassed about a wealth that had never been expected. He wondered if he needed a change. Exploring his strengths and himself in flow reinforced that he was in the right area of work but that did not help him. He felt trapped by a success that increasingly he felt he did not deserve, because it had never been planned. In answering the five whys he revealed:

Why he went to work?
To earn money.
Why did he want to do that?
To pay for his children being privately educated.
Why did he want to do that?
So that they would have a good start in life.
Why did he want to do that?
Because his parents had not been able to do that for him, and he had floundered for years before finding what he wanted to do.
Why did he want to do that?
Because having confidence in yourself and your abilities is the gift he most wanted to give his children.
Why did he want to do that?
Because he wanted to be the best father he could be not only for their childhood, but for their whole life.

Knowing that his desire for money was linked to more than seeing his bank balance grow, that it was intimately connected with being a good father who gave his children confidence in themselves that would equip them for life; re-energized his connection with work. It highlighted that money was more than a means of buying education. He now knew what purpose his success had, and with that he was able to start linking himself to devising a strategy for business growth. The doing became easier once it was linked to his being.

Talking of purpose and meaning can lead into issues of spirituality. Spirituality is something coaches are often reluctant to discuss with clients. As a largely secular society, spirituality has become an invisible part of experience, particularly within work. Some clients prefer to keep their religious beliefs private, perhaps sensing their coach does not share their faith. Enquiries as to spirituality can be heard as meaning religious faith, and the client may profess to hold none. Decoupling spirituality from religion and linking it to the importance of people finding meaning in how they live their life, enables it to be seen as one of the personal constructs that drives individual decision-making. It allows for the 'who am I?' question to be part of the coaching work. Some coaches are very comfortable in this territory. Constructivist exploration of life themes can be used to explore individual purpose and meaning. Alternatively, a tool such as Signpost Cards (available from www. innovative resources. org.) offers visual images as prompts for discussions about meaning and significance.

Stretchability

Stretchability is different from flexibility. Where flexibility is about moving with the prevailing winds, stretchability is about being willing to reach out beyond a comfort point in order to touch something new. People I have experienced as being career resilient have often had to let go of skills and experience because they recognize that their value is declining against the emerging context. It is difficult to acknowledge that something one loves is not going to equip you for what is developing ahead. Looking at change from a business perspective, PESTLE allows for assessing individual currency value: for assessing what in a portfolio of skills, knowledge, and experience is becoming of less value and what is becoming of increasing value. It also identifies when a new currency needs to be acquired. This is more than putting together a personal development plan. It is about looking at what can be leveraged, and what needs to be rested. It is about stretching to match with what is, rather than what was.

Stretching contact

Stretchability is also about being able to reach out to people who have the power to give the client what they want, and being able to do so in ways that are authentic and meaningful to them. Mention the word 'networking' and most clients will admit they know they should, while their facial expression signals their distaste. 'Your network is your net worth' has become a motto of the digital age. This means showing enthusiasm for both virtual and physical connection. While networking gives encouragement to extroverts to increase an activity they enjoy, it increases guilt in introverts for failing to do so. The wide netcasting approach also fails to address the core issue of the quality of the contact. Networking for career resilience is about having conversations that are designed to pull the other person into wanting connection, rather than pushing connection onto them. Some years ago, I conducted research on how women executives in a number of countries networked. This was driven by reading books on networking, which did not accord with what I observed when at international meetings. In separating out nationalities, I discovered that Americans were comfortable with a transactional model based on both parties assessing their mutual career value and then making a decision as to whether to maintain contact. Mediterranean colleagues operated a relational model where enjoyment of social contact was the test as to whether any business contact would follow. While British women simply felt embarassed by the idea that they should make themselves known to more powerful players, and then felt uncertain as to how to use the connection when they did. The British model was one of gauche reluctance. I did not repeat the research with men, but I suspect many of the same themes would have emerged. My UK research participants claimed they did not know what to do with a contact to make it into something meaningful. What they did not recognize was that it is through contact that problems in our wider life get solved. It is our network of friends and neighbours who tell us who is the best doctor, which plumber is reliable, and who will offer to trade childcare. It is no different in work, if people do not know that your client has a skill that could be of value in dealing with a problem, then that is a personal and a business waste. Stretching a network may not be about making it bigger, but about making it stronger by engaging in different forms of conversation. When working with clients who know that they should network but fail to act because of discomfort in being seen as pushy, invite them to engage in reconnaissance gathering by talking with people to discover what is going on in their part of the business, what challenges they face, what is proving difficult to deliver on, and what they would like to have available to them that would make a difference.

In focusing on the other person, the client stops seeing themselves as a poor salesman and can begin to focus on listening. They can have a conversation where the questions they ask display their skills and experience. If their skills and experience are relevant, it may lead to a new role or project. If their skills and experience are not relevant, they have still had a meaningful conversation, which allowed them to be authentic, and which may be of value for the future.

Stretching oneself

Stretch is about a willingness to move outside of existing boundaries and to take risks. We saw that in Alastair's account of the impact of his bank being acquired. He saw the changes that were coming from acquisition, but he did more than adapt who he was to the new environment. He stretched himself into unknown territory in the hope it would give him a career springboard. Helping a client to recognize how stretchable they are is an important part of resilience. Stretch too far and the elastic breaks; stretch too little and they may not be able to accommodate the shape the organization is now taking.

Having worked through the emerging future and its implications for flexibility, and core areas of stability, the final dimension is tolerance for stretch.

Exercise 10.2: The stretchability exercise

Invite your client to write down on postcards the key ideas that have come out of your work together. That work may have encompassed work on strengths, values, life themes, motivations, as well as changes in their career context. Ask them to record one idea per postcard. Encourage them to claim as many ideas as they can.

Once they have captured their thoughts, lay all the postcards out and invite them to choose any three at random. In looking at those three, what idea does it generate as to what they might do. This may encompass new ideas about the sort of work they could do, how they work, actions to be taken inside or outside of their existing organization, or development to be acquired.

Repeat the process of random selection of three cards as prompts for idea generation until the ideas are exhausted or the same ideas are being repeated, regardless of the card combination.

Lay out the ideas they have generated. Now offer them a balloon and ask them to inflate the balloon to the point at which they become uncomfortable at blowing any more air in. This is the limit of their stretchability. When they look again at their ideas, which idea represents the limits of their stretchability? Which ideas are within the scope of their stretch, and which lie outside? There is no judgement attached to their stretch point, it is simply data that this is as far as they are likely to want to stretch. Some clients will blow to the point of bursting, others will stop when the balloon looks half empty. Being honest about stretchability allows the client to let go of what they should be or do, and work with what they can be or do.

Using a balloon is a useful visual tool, because it makes visible the degree of stretch a person has available to them. Where a client has a fear of balloons, then a strong elastic band or exercise band can serve the same purpose. The exercise allows for recognizing that even though a client accepts realities and can flex, they will have limits to their stretchability, and that needs to be worked with.

Flex, stretch, and stabilize

Flexibility, stretchability, and stability are the three dimensions of individual career resilience. They are like the three mirrors that reside inside a kaleidoscope. Clients bring to career coaching the kaleidoscope pattern they have become familiar with. Their resilience is increased when the coach helps them shake up the pieces so that a new pattern can form, and they do so with the knowledge that their career will continue to form new patterns throughout their working life. The client holds the kaleidoscope as their career container but will be unable to predict with certainty what patterns will take shape. Increasing their resilience equips them to work with those changes and to recognize the possibilities of change.

Summary

In this final chapter on resilience, the focus has turned to career resilience, as a distinct need for clients. It has done this through:

- Looking at career theories of the twentieth century and recognizing how twenty-first-century clients are often operating from last century models.
- Identifying career constructivism and chaos theory as two relevant theories for working with the reality of careers.
- Recognizing that career resilience seen simply as a set of actions that provide protection against the vicissitudes of the employment market ignores the need to have an internalized sense of resilience before being able to take resilient actions.
- Offering career resilience as a model of flexibility, stability, and stretchability.
- Providing additional materials particular to career conversations.

Bibliography

Alford, B.A. and Beck, A.T. (1998) *The Integrative Power of Cognitive Therapy*. New York: Guilford Press.

Borg, T., Bright, J.E.H. and Pryor, R.G.L. (2006) The Butterfly Model of careers: illustrating how planning and chance can be integrated into the careers of high school students, *Australian Journal of Career Development*, 15 (3): 53–8.

Brann, A. (2015) *Neuroscience for Coaches*. London: Kogan Page.

Brown, P. and Brown, V. (2012) *Neuropsychology for Coaches*. Maidenhead: Open University Press.

Campbell, J. (2009) *Resilience: Personal and organisational summary findings* [http://www.lifetimeswork.com/assets/documents/Insights/Insight%204%20Resilience%20Summary%20FINAL.pdf].

Carter, O.L., Presti, D.E., Callistemon, C., Ungerer, Y., Liu, G.B. and Pettigrew, J.D. (2005) Meditation alters perceptual rivalry in Tibetan Buddhist monks, *Current Biology*, 15: 412–13.

Casserley, T. and Megginson, D. (2009) *Learning from Burnout*. Oxford: Elsevier.

Chartered Institute of Personnel and Development (CIPD) (2014a) *Megatrends: Are we working harder than ever*. London: CIPD.

Chartered Institute of Personnel and Development (CIPD) (2014b) *Employee Outlook*. London: CIPD.

Chaskalson, M. (2011) *The Mindful Workplace: Developing resilient individuals and resonant organisations with MBSR*. Chichester: Wiley-Blackwell.

Csikszentmihalyi, M. (1997) *Finding Flow: The psychology of engagement with everyday life*. New York: Basic Books.

Davidson, R.J., Kabat-Zinn, J. and Schumacher, J. (2003) Alterations in brain and immune functions produced by mindfulness meditation, *Psychosomatic Medicine*, 65: 564–70.

De Shazer, S. (1988) *Clues: Investigating solutions in brief therapy*. New York: Norton.

De Shazer, S., Berg, I.K., Lipchik, E., Molnar, A., Gingerich, W. and Weiner-Davis, M. (1986) Brief therapy: focussed solution development, *Family Process*,25: 207–21.

Drake, D.B. (2004) Creating third space: the use of narrative liminality in coaching, in I. Stein, F. Campone and L.J. Page (eds.) *Proceedings of the Second ICF Coaching Research Symposium*. Lexington, KY: ICF.

Driver, M. (2011) *Coaching Positively: Lessons for coaches from positive psychology*. Maidenhead: Open University Press.

Egeland, B., Carlson, E. and Straufe, L.A. (1993) Resilience as a process, *Development and Psychopathology*,5: 517–28.

Ellis, A. (1962) *Reason and Emotion in Psychotherapy*. New York: Lyle Stuart.

Fletcher, D. and Sarkar, M. (2012) A grounded theory of psychological resilience in Olympic champions, *Psychology of Sport and Exercise*, 13: 669–728.

Fredrickson, B. (2011) *Positivity: Ground breaking research to release your inner optimist and thrive*. New York: Random House.

Fredrickson, B.L. and Losada, M.L. (2005) Positive affect and complex dynamics of human flourishing, *American Psychologist*, 60 (7): 678–86.

Fredrickson, B.L., Tugade, M.M., Waugh, C.E. and Larkin, G.R. (2003) What good are positive emotions in crises? A prospective study of resilience and emotions following the terrorist attacks on the United States on September 11th 2001, *Journal of Personality and Social Psychology*, 84 (3): 365–76.

Freudenberger, H.J. (1974) Staff burnout, *Journal of Social Issues*, 30 (1): 159–65.

Graham, L. (2013) *Bouncing Back: Rewiring your brain for maximum resilience and well-being*.Novato, CA: New World Library.

Grepmair, L., Mitterlehner, F., Loew, T. and Bachler, E. (2007) Promoting mindfulness in psychotherapists in training influences the treatment results of their patients: a randomised double blind controlled study, *Psychotherapy and Psychosomatics*, 76 (6): 332–8.

Hall, L. (2013) *Mindful Coaching: How mindfulness can transform coaching practice*. London: Kogan Page.

Harris, R. (2006) Embrace your demons: an overview of Acceptance and Commitment Therapy, *Psychotherapy in Australia*, 12 (4): 2–8 [http://www.actmindfully.com.au/upimages/Dr_Russ_Harris_-_A_Non-technical_Overview_of_ACT.pdf].

Harris, R. (2008) *The Happiness Trap*. London: Robinson.

Harris, R. (2009) *ACT Made Simple*. Oakland, CA: New Harbinger Press.

Harris, R. (2012) *The Reality Gap*. London: Robinson.

Hayes, S.C. and Smith, S. (2005) *Get Out of Your Mind and Into Your Life*. Oakland, CA: New Harbinger Press.

Hebb, D.O. (2002) *The Organization of Behavior: A neuropsychological theory*.London: Taylor & Francis.

Hodgkinson, P.E. and Stewart, M. (1991) *The Handbook of Disaster Management*. London: Routledge.

Humphrey, J. and Green, A. (2012) *Coaching for Resilience*. London: Kogan Page.

Ivesen, C., George, E. and Ratner, H. (2012) *Brief Coaching: A solutions focused approach*. Hove: Routledge.

Jackson, P.Z. and McKergow, M. (2002) *The Solutions Focus*. London: Nicholas Brealey.

Jepsen, D.A. and Choudhuri, (2001) Stability and change in 25-year career occupational career patterns, *Career Development Quarterly*, 50: 3–19.

Jha, A.P., Stanley, E.A., Kiyonaga, A., Wong, L. and Gelford, L. (2010) Examining the protective effects of mindfulness training on working memory capacity and affective experience, *Emotion*, 10 (1): 54–64.

Kabat-Zinn, J. (1991) *Full Catastrophe Living: Using the wisdom of your body and mind to face stress, pain and illness*. New York: Delta.

Kabat-Zinn, J. (2005) *Coming to Our Senses: Healing ourselves and the world through mindfulness*. London: Piatkus.

Kegan, R. and Lahey, L. (2009) *Immunity to Change*. Cambridge, MA: Harvard University Press.

Killingsworth, M.A. and Gilbert, D.T. (2010) A wandering mind is an unhappy mind, *Science*, 330 (6006): 932.

Linley, A., Willars, J. and Biswas-Dienar, R. (2010) *The Strengths Book: Be confident, be successful and enjoy better relationships*. Coventry: CAPP Press.

Lorenz, E. (1993) *The Essence of Chaos*. Seattle: WA: University of Washington Press.

Masten, A.S. (2001) Ordinary magic: resilience processes in development, *American Psychologist*, 56: 227–38.

Mental Health Foundation (2010) *Be Mindful*. London: Mental Health Foundation.

Padesky, C.A. and Mooney, K.A. (2012) Strengths based cognitive behavioural therapy: a four step model to build resilience, *Journal of Clinical Psychology and Psychotherapy*, 19: 283–90.

Pals, J. (2006) Constructing the springboard effect: causal connections, self-making and growth within the life story, in D.P. McAdams, R. Josselson and A. Lieblich (eds.) *Identity and Story*. Washington, DC: American Psychological Association.

Pemberton, C. (2006a) *Coaching to Solutions*. Oxford: Butterworth Heinemann.

Pemberton, C. (2006b) *Strike a New Career Deal*. London: Pearson.

Pemberton, C. (2014) *Understanding resilience within the professional practice of a coach*.Unpublished DProf, Middlesex University.

Pennebaker, J.W. (1993) Putting stress into words: health, linguistic and therapeutic implications, *Behavior Research and Therapy*, 31: 539–48.

Pennebaker, J.W. (1997) Writing about emotional experiences as a therapeutic process, *Psychological Science*, 8 (3): 162–6.

Pryor, R. and Bright, J. (2011) The *Chaos Theory of Careers*. London: Routledge.

Rath, T. (2007) *StrengthsFinder2.0*. New York: Gallup Press.

Redmond, A. and Crisafulli, P. (2010) *Comebacks*. San Francisco, CA: Jossey-Bass.

Reivich, K. and Shatté, A. (2002) *The Resilience Factor*. New York: Broadway Books.

Rowe, G., Hirsh, J.B. and Anderson, A.K. (2007) Positive affect increases the breadth of affective selection, *Proceedings of the National Academy of Sciences of the United States of America*, 104: 383–8.

Rutter, M. (1985) Resistance in the face of adversity: protective factors and resistance to psychiatric disorders, *British Journal of Psychiatry*, 147: 598–611.

Sarkar, M. and Fletcher, D. (2014) Ordinary magic, extraordinary performance: psychological resilience and thriving in high achievers, *Sport, Exercise and Performance Psychology*,3 (1): 46–60.

Sartre, J. (2000)*The Words*. London: Penguin.

Savickas, M. (2011) *Career Counseling*. Washington, DC: American Psychological Association.

Seligman, M.E.P. (2011) What business can learn from a pioneering army program for fostering post-traumatic growth, *Harvard Business Review*, 89 (4): 101–16.

Seligman, M.E.P. and Csikszentmihalyi, M. (2000) Positive psychology: an introduction, *Special edition of the American Psychologist*, 55 (1): 5–14.

Sliding Doors (1998) London: Miramax Films (UK).

Smyth, J. (1998) Written emotional expression: effect sizes, outcome types, and moderating variables, *Journal of Consulting and Clinical Psychology*, 66: 174–84.

Southwick, S.M. and Charney, D.S. (2012) *Resilience: The science of mastering life's greatest challenges*. Cambridge: Cambridge University Press.

Spence, G.G., Cavanagh, M.J. and Grant, A.M. (2008) The integration of mindfulness training and health coaching: an exploratory study, *Coaching: An International Journal of Theory and Practice*, 1 (2): 145–63.

Spera, S.P., Buhrfiend, D.D. and Pennebaker, J.W. (1994) Expressive writing and coping with job loss, *Academy of Management Journal*, 37: 722–33.

Tehrani, N., Cox, S.J. and Cox, T. (2002) Assessing the impact of stressful incidents in organisations: the development of an extended impact of events scale, *Counselling Psychology Quarterly*, 15 (2): 191–200.

The Full Monty (1997) London: Twentieth Century Fox (UK).

VIA Institute Survey is available on line at http://www.viacharacter.org/www/Character-Strengths/Personality-Assessment#nav

Waddell, M. (1994) *Owl Babies*. London: Walker Books.

Werner, E. and Smith, R.S. (1977) *Kauia's Children Come of Age*. Hawaii: University of Hawaii Press.

Williams, M. and Penman, D. (2011) *Mindfulness: A practical guide to finding peace in a frantic world*. London: Piatkus.

Woods, K., Bond, C., Humphrey, N., Symes, W. and Green, L. (2011) *Systematic Review of Solution Focused Brief Therapy (SFBT) with Children and Families*. Research Report DFE-RR179, Department of Education [https://www.gov.uk/government/uploads/system/uploads/attachment_data/file/184113/DFE-RR179.pdf].

Index

[Page numbers in **bold** refer to tables; those in *italics* refer to figures]

ABC model 57–63
  challenging ABC **60**
  examples of ABC **60**
  vs. CBT 61–3
acceptance and commitment
    therapy 66–79
  acceptance/opening up 75–6
  client core pathologies 70–71
  committed action 78
  connecting with value 76–8
  contacting present moment 71–2
  definition 67–8
  defusion 73–5
  relevance to resilience 66–7
  when ACT is right choice 78–9
  when we cannot be present 68–70
access to identity 10
access to resilience 25
ACT *see* acceptance and
    commitment therapy
ACTH 17
adjustment 44
adrenaline 6–7, 17
adult experiences 11–12
adversity 57
'aha' moments 83
AIDS 5

alchemy 38
American Psychological Association
    109–110
amygdala 6–7
analysis of coaching sessions 44
anxiety 6–8, 68–9, 74, 79, 82–6, 107
APA *see* American Psychological
    Association
application of mindfulness 80–81
attachment to conceptualized self
    70–71
Attenborough, David 59
authenticity 86
autonomy 7, 33, 39, 70, 121, 126
avoidance 14–15

Baldwin, Neil 109
Bank of England 55–6
basal ganglia 48
Beck, Aaron 52, 54
beliefs 57
Berg, Insoo Kim 95–6
bipolar disorders 63
blaming 55, 67
blind optimism 24
Borg, Tony 132–3
bounceback 2–3

Bowlby, John 7–8
braking 44
Brann, Amy 48, 83
breaking habits 92–3
breathing mindfully 87–9
brief therapy 96, 100
Bright, Jim 128–9, 133
broadening and building 111, 115
Brown, Paul 83
Brown, Virginia 83
Buddhism 67, 80–83
burnout 1, 13–19, 79
    dimensions of 16–19
butterfly model 127, 132–3

Campbell, Jenny 12
capacity building 13
Career Butterfly in Action *133*
Career Butterfly Model *133*
career constructivism 125–7
    criticism of constructivism 126–7
career development theory 124–5
career resilience 12–13, 122–39
    coaching for 122–39
    different perspective on 12–13
Career Resilience Model 130–31,
    130
caring 76–7
case studies
    career constructivism 126
    career growth through
        uncertainty 129
    cautionary tale of mindfulness 86
    coaching 4 steps model 62–3
    connecting with values 77–8
    finding the exception 106
    Five Whys 134–5
    hearing narrative 39
    introducing mindfulness 85
    mindfulness of breathing 90–91
    Miracle Question 104
    opening up to stop 75–6
    positivity/creativity 116

recognizing client template 4
recognizing PTSD 15–16
second narrative 36
separating from the thought 74–5
solution-focused questioning 98
sustaining a story 49–50
trusting the flow 113–14
unearthing identity 33–4
working with ABC 58
working positively with
    negativity 120
working the scale 99–100
Casserley, Tim 16
caveats on mindfulness 84–5
CBT *see* cognitive behavioural
    therapy
challenging ABC **60**
chance 128–9
change 42–3, 129–30
    increasing openness to 129–30
    tolerance for 129
chaos theory 127–9
Chartered Institute of Personnel
    and Development 2, 122
Chaskalson, Michael 89
Churchill, Winston 50
CIPD *see* Chartered Institute of
    Personnel and Development
clarifying values 77
client as cause of problem 55
client as expert 96–7
client template 4
coach in the coaching process *46*
coaching for career resilience
    122–39
    career constructivism 125–7
    career development theory 124–5
    career resilience 130–31
    chaos theory 127
    fitting person to job 123–4
    flex-stability ratio 128
    flex/stretch/stabilize 139
    flexibility 131–3

increasing openness to change 129–30
stability 134–6
stretchability 136–8
tolerance for change 129
working with chance 128–9
coaching the narrative 41–51
immunity to change 42–3
Narrative Wave™ 43–5
reinforcers 50–51
role of coach 46–8
sustaining narrative 48
sustaining a story 49–50
when client is in story 45–6
cognitive behavioural therapy xii, 52–65, 111
CBT vs. ABC 61–3
definition 52–3
distorted thinking 56–7
introducing CBT framework 59–61
relevance to resilience 53
thinking after resilience loss 54–6
when CBT is not right choice 63–4
working within CBT framework 57–9
cognitive processing 31, 82
coherence 37
collusion 75–6, 97
committed action 78
competence 121
concept of career resilience 130–31
conceptualized self 70–71
connecting 76–7, 121
connecting with values 76–8
consequence 57
contacting present 71–2
contentment 110
contributing 76–7
coping strategies 75–6
core belief systems 52
core pathologies of client 70–71
corporate high achievers 5, 12

cortisol 17
cravings 17
creating mindful habits 91–2
creating personal resilience model 61
creativity 116
Crisafulli, Patricia 66–7
criticisms of CBT 63–4
criticisms of constructivism 126–7
criticisms of positivity 119–20
Csikszentmihalyi, Mihalyi 112

dartboard exercise 76–7
Davidson, Richard 82–3
day-dreaming 83
de Shazar, Steve 95–6, 103
definitions
acceptance and commitment therapy 67–8
cognitive behavioural therapy 52–3
mindfulness 80–81
positive psychology 109–110
resilience 1–2
solution-focused coaching 95–6
defusion 73–5
naming story 73–4
neutralizing 74–5
noticing 73
Department of Education 107
depression 63–4, 79, 107, 119
detachment 15
different perspective on career resilience 12–13
dimensions of burnout 16–19
dimensions of career resilience 139
dimensions of PTSD 14–16
avoidance 14–15
increased arousal 15–16
reliving 14
distorted thinking 54–7
due to loss of resilience 54–6
working with 56–7

dominance of past/future 69, 71
Drake, David 38
dulling the sense 4
dynamism 99–100
dyslexia 95

effect of mindfulness on brain 82–4
elasticity 2, 22–3, 131
Ellis, Albert 52
emotional control 22, 24
empathy 46, 96, 115
entering 44
Epictetus 52–3
equilibrium 7
ethics 20
eustress 112
evidence of power of mindfulness 82
examples of ABC **60**
exiting 44
experiential avoidance 69, 71

facing reality 67
fairy stories 30, 104
fantasizing 69, 71
fatigue 17
finding exception 97, 105–6
fitting person to position 123–4
Five Whys 134–5
5HTT gene 6
Fletcher, David 11
flex-stability ratio 128
flexibility 131–3
    flexing to external world 131–2
    personal 132–3
flexing to external world 131–2
flow 111–15
fMRI scans 82–3
focus on future 97
focusing on breath 87–91
following breath 89–90
forms of narrative 37–8
4 Ss model 102–3

4 steps model 61–3
    creating personal resilience model 61
    maintaining resilience 62
    practising resilience 62–3
    unpicking action 61
framework of CBT 57–9
    introducing 59–61
    working within 57–9
Fredrickson, Barbara 111, 115, 117
Freudenberger, Herbert 17
Full Monty 66
fusion 69–70
future focus 97

Gallup StrengthsFinder 114
generalizing 55
genetics 6–7
Gilbert, Daniel 81
goal-setting 48, 103–5
Google 42
Graham, Linda 83
gratitude 115, 120–21
Green, Adrienne 56
grounding 71–2

habit-breaking 92–3
habits of mindfulness 91–2
Hall, Liz 89
Hanson, Rick 81
Harris, Russ 71–2
Harvard Business School 42
Hayes, Steven 67
Hebb, Donald 50
helplessness 56
Henley, William Ernest 50
history of resilience 5
Hodgkinson, Peter 14
holding 44
holding wave pattern *45*
HPA axis *see* hypothalamic-pituitary-adrenal axis

humour 16, 61
Humphrey, John 56
hyper-vigilance 15, 18
hypothalamic-pituitary-adrenal
    axis 17

identity 32–4
immunity to change 42–3
importance of authenticity 86
inability to be in present 68–70
    attachment to conceptualized
        self 70
    dominance of past/future 69
    experiential avoidance 69
    fusion 69
    lack of certainty over values
        69–70
    unworkable actions 70
incident impact 34–5
increased arousal 15–16
increasing openness to change
    129–30
incrementalism 99, 101
inevitability of suffering 67
infertility 24
intermediate writing 36–7

jumping ahead 54

Kabat-Zinn, Jon 80–82
Keele University 109
Keenan, Brian 53
Kegan, Robert 42
Killingsworth, Matthew 81
knowledge of resilience 5

lack of certainty over values
    69–70
Lahey, Lisa 42
learning and resilience coaching
    28
lenses for working with resilience
    12

life events 2, 10, 24–5
life's curve ball 53, 70
limitations of mindfulness 84–5
link between mindfulness and
    resilience 81–2
link between resilience and written
    narrative 31
LinkedIn 4
Linley, Alex 114
Lorenz, Edward 127
Losada, Marcial 115–16
losing resilience 3–5, 10
    access to identity 10
    recognition of 3–5
loss of access to identity 10
loss of function 63–4
loss of resilience narrative 29–40,
    125
    intermediate writing 36–7
    link between resilience and
        written narrative 31
    narrative and identity 32–4
    story-telling 30
    structuring narrative 34–5
    two narratives 37–8
    value of repeated writing 35–6
    working with client narrative
        38–40
    writing in the moment 31–2
Lundgren, Tobias 76–7

McKee, Annie 81–2
maintaining resilience 25, 62
Mandela, Nelson 50
Maslow, Abraham 109
Masten, Ann 8
MBSR *see* Mindfulness Based Stress
    Reduction programme
'Me plc' 130
meaning 22–3
Megatrends 2
Mental Health Foundation (UK) 82
mental illness 5, 109–110

mindfulness 80–94
  breaking habits 92–3
  creating mindful habits 91–2
  definition 80–81
  evidence for power of
    mindfulness 82
  importance of authenticity 86
  limitations of 84–5
  link with resilience 81–2
  what mindfulness does to brain
    82–4
  when mindfulness is not answer
    93
  working with 87–91
Mindfulness Based Stress Reduction
  programme 82
Miracle Question 103–5
motivation 42, 51, 61, 99, 113–17,
  134, 138

naming story 73–4
narrative of resilience 29–40
  see also coaching the narrative
Narrative Wave™ 43–5, *43*, 48
National Health Service 53, 84
networking 136–7
neural plasticity 7, 83
neuropeptides 6
neuroscience 6, 42, 48, 81, 83–4
neutralizing 74–5
NHS *see* National Health Service
9/11 115
noticing 73

obsessiveness 84
Ockham's Razor 97–8
'OKness' 12
Olympic Games 11–12
opening up 75–6
  see also acceptance and
    commitment therapy
openness to change 26, 129–30
optimism 7, 10, 24, 110, 129

'ordinary magic' 8
origins of 'resilience' 1–2
over-zealous negativity 119
overachieving 17
  see also burnout

Padesky, Christine 61
Pals, Jennifer 31
Parsons, Frank 123–5
partial vision 54
Penman, Danny 89
Penn Resiliency Program 110
Pennebaker, James 31
permanent thinking 56
Perry, William 42
personal flexibility 132–3
personal resilience 20–28
  benchmark position of 24
  reflecting on coaching 27–8
  resilience in coaching 26
  Resilience Questionnaire 21–2
  resultant profiles from the
    questionnaire 23–4
  scoring the questionnaire 22
  taking learning back into
    coaching 28
  when going gets tough 24–6
personal thinking 57
pervasive thinking 57
pessimism 10, 110
PESTLE model 131–2, 136
  analysis **132**
positioning of problem 100–101
positive emergence 36
positive psychology xii, 109–121
  broadening/building 111
  creativity 116
  criticisms of 119–20
  definition 109–110
  flow 111–15
  gratitude 120–21
  positivity 115–16
  relevance to resilience 110–111

when it is right choice 121
  working with positivity 117–19
positivity 24, 115–16
  realistic 24
Positivity Ratio Checklist *118*
post-traumatic stress disorder 1,
    13–19, 24, 79
  dimensions of 14–16
power of emotion 5
power of mindfulness 82
power of Miracle Question 103–5
practising resilience 62–3
presence in narrative 45–6
principles of CBT xii
principles of positive psychology
    110–111
principles of solution-focused
    coaching 96–101
  client as expert 96–7
  find exception 97
  future focus 97
  not problem phobic 100–101
  progress in small steps 99–100
  question with simplicity 97–8
proactivity 22, 24, 48
problem phobia 100–101
procrastination 3
profiles from Resilience
    Questionnaire 23–4
  elasticity 23
  emotional control 24
  meaning 23
  proactivity 24
  realistic positivity 24
  self-belief 23
  solution finding 23
  support 23
progress in small steps 99–100
prophecy 55–6
protection 7–8, 13
  building 13
Pryor, Robert 128–9, 133
psychological health 9

psychological inflexibility
    68–70
psychological integrity 14
psychometric testing 6
PTSD *see* post-traumatic stress
    disorder
public stories 29–30

Queen Elizabeth II, 55–6
questioning with simplicity 97–8

rape 14
realistic positivity 22, 24, 26
recognition of loss of resilience
    3–5
recognizing when client is in story
    45–6
Redmond, Andrea 66–7
REFLECT indicators of strengths
    114–15
reflecting on coaching 27–8
reflective comparison 25–6
reframing 68
reinforcers 50–51
relational frame theory 67–8
relevance of ACT to resilience 66–7
relevance of CBT to resilience 53
relevance of positive psychology to
    resilience 110–111
reliving 14
Renaissance 127
renewal 13
repeated writing 35–6
resilience 10–11
resilience in coaching 26
Resilience Engine™ 12
resilience gaps xiv, 63–4
resilience narrative 29–40
  loss of 29–40
resilience as process 8–9
Resilience Questionnaire 21–2, **21**,
    25
resilience template 101–3, *103*

resilience vs. PTSD and burnout
13–19
burnout 16–19
post-traumatic stress disorder
14–16
resiliency 10–11, 24
resources toolkit 26
RFT *see* relational frame theory
Rogers, Carl 109
role of coach 46–8
Roosevelt, Eleanor 24

sagacity 102
Sarkar, Mustafa 11
Sartre, Jean Paul 29
Savickas, Mark 125
scale creation *100*
scaling 99–100
scoring Resilience Questionnaire 22
secure attachment 7–8
self-anaesthetizing x
self-assessment 117
self-belief 13, 22–3, 48, 99–100, 129
self-confidence 2–4, 7
self-criticism 27, 114
self-defeating behaviours 67–8
self-efficacy 55
self-esteem 66
self-marketing 13
self-protection 13
self-reflection 37
self-stretching 137–8
self-worth 107
Seligman, Martin 109–111
sense of purpose 27–8
serotonin 6–7
shadow identity 47
Signpost Cards 136
skills 102
Sliding Doors 128
small steps for progress 99–100
Smith, R.S. 7
Smyth, Joshua 31–2

social media 13
solution finding 22–3
solution-focused coaching xii,
95–108
definition 95–6
principles of 96–101
value of approach 101
when it is right choice 107–8
working with approach 101–6
solution-focused questioning 98
spirituality 135–6
stability 13–14, 134–6
Stewart, Michael 14
Stoke City Football Club 109
stopping 75–6
story-telling 30, 37–8
strategies 102
Stress Reduction Clinic (UMMC) 80
stretchability 136–8
stretching contact 136–7
stretching oneself 137–8
stretching contact 136–7
structuring narrative 34–5
'stuckness' xiii
studying mindfulness 82–4
Sufism 81
Super, Donald 123–5
support 22–3, 44, 102
survivors of extreme conditions 5
sustainability 48, 53
sustaining narrative 48
sustaining a story 49–50
sympathetic nervous system 17

taking learning into resilience
coaching 28
Taoism 81
tasks of coach 46–8
Tehrani, Nohreen 16
Teleos Leadership Institute 82
testing resilience 24
losing access to resilience 25
reflective comparison 25

remaining resilient 25
self-image 25–6
thinking changes when resilience
    goes 54–6
    blaming 55
    client as cause of problem 55
    generalizing 55
    jumping ahead 54
    partial vision 54
    prophecy 55–6
    using wrong lens 54–5
third space 38
three-factor model of resilience 9
3:1 ratio 115–17, 119
3 Ps 56–7
time-limited coaching 80
tolerance for change 129
Tolle, Eckhart 82
Toronto University 116
trait theory 6–7
2-adrenoreceptor gene 6
'twoness' 100

uncertainty 36, 74, 129
unearthing exception 32, 97, 105–6
unpicking action 61
unworkable actions 70–71
US Army 110–111
using wrong lens 54–5

value of repeated writing 35–6
value of solution-focused coaching
    101
values 69–71, 76–8
    connecting with 76–8
    dartboard 77
Values in Action 110–111
values dartboard 77
ViA see Values in Action
Vocational Bureau 123

Wellspring Institute for
    Neuroscience 81

Werner, E. 7
what ACT is 67–8
what CBT is 52–3
what positive psychology is
    109–110
what resilience is 1–19
    career resilience 12–13
    corporate high achievers 12
    definition 1–2
    lenses for working with resilience
        13
    losing resilience 3–5, 10
    loss of access to identity 10
    protection 7–8
    resilience as process 8–9
    resilience and resiliency 10–11
    thinking about resilience 5
    trait theory 6–7
    vs. PTSD and burnout 13–19
    what it is not 2–3
    working with adults 11–12
    working with resilience factors
        9–10
what resilience is not 2–3
what solution-focused coaching is
    95–6
when ACT is right choice 78–9
when going gets tough 24–6
when mindfulness is not right
    choice 93
when positive psychology is right
    choice 121
when solution-focused approach is
    right choice 107–8
William of Ockham 97–8
Williams, Mark 89
working with chance 128–9
working with client narrative 38–40
working with distorted thinking
    56–7
    permanent 56
    personal 57
    pervasive 57

working with mindfulness 87–91
   focusing on breath 87–91
working with positivity 117–19
working with solution-focused
     coaching 101–6
   power of Miracle Question 103–5
   resilience template 101–3
   unearth the exception 105–6
working with three-factor model 9–10

working within CBT framework
   57–9
   ABC model 57–8
writing in the moment 31–2
written narrative 31

your resilience 20–28
   see also personal resilience

COACHING POSITIVELY
Lessons for Coaches from Positive Psychology

Matt Driver

9780335241156 (Paperback)
July 2011

eBook also available

Coaching is a positive practice which focuses on building people's resourcefulness and positive beliefs about themselves. Recent research into positive psychology supports and builds upon current coaching practice and also refines it.Like many other coaches, managers and consultants, Matt Driver has found this relatively new field to be inspiring and to offer practical insights into his work. It is proving to be of enormous value to people who are interested in what works rather than what does not and who aim to fulfil themselves by developing their natural strengths.

Key features:

- Brings together substantial psychological research
- Includes examples from coaching clients that shows what has worked best for them
- Stresses the importance of relationships, autonomy and achievement in the coaching process

www.openup.co.uk

Coaching Behind Bars
Facing challenges and putting hope in a womens prison.

Clare McGregor

ISBN: 978-0-335-26442-1 (Paperback)
eBook: 978-0-335-26443-8
2015

Most people's perception of coaching is that it is a high value service for highly paid executives or managers. But what if you offered it to some of the most marginalized people in our society - women in prison? This inspirational book describes how Clare McGregor set out to do just that. Reading it, you will find a lot of your preconceptions about prisons and prisoners challenged. The book celebrates the amazing resilience of the human spirit.

Book chapters include:

- Welcome to HMP & YOI Styal
- What do you want to change?
- Through the gate and beyond

www.openup.co.uk